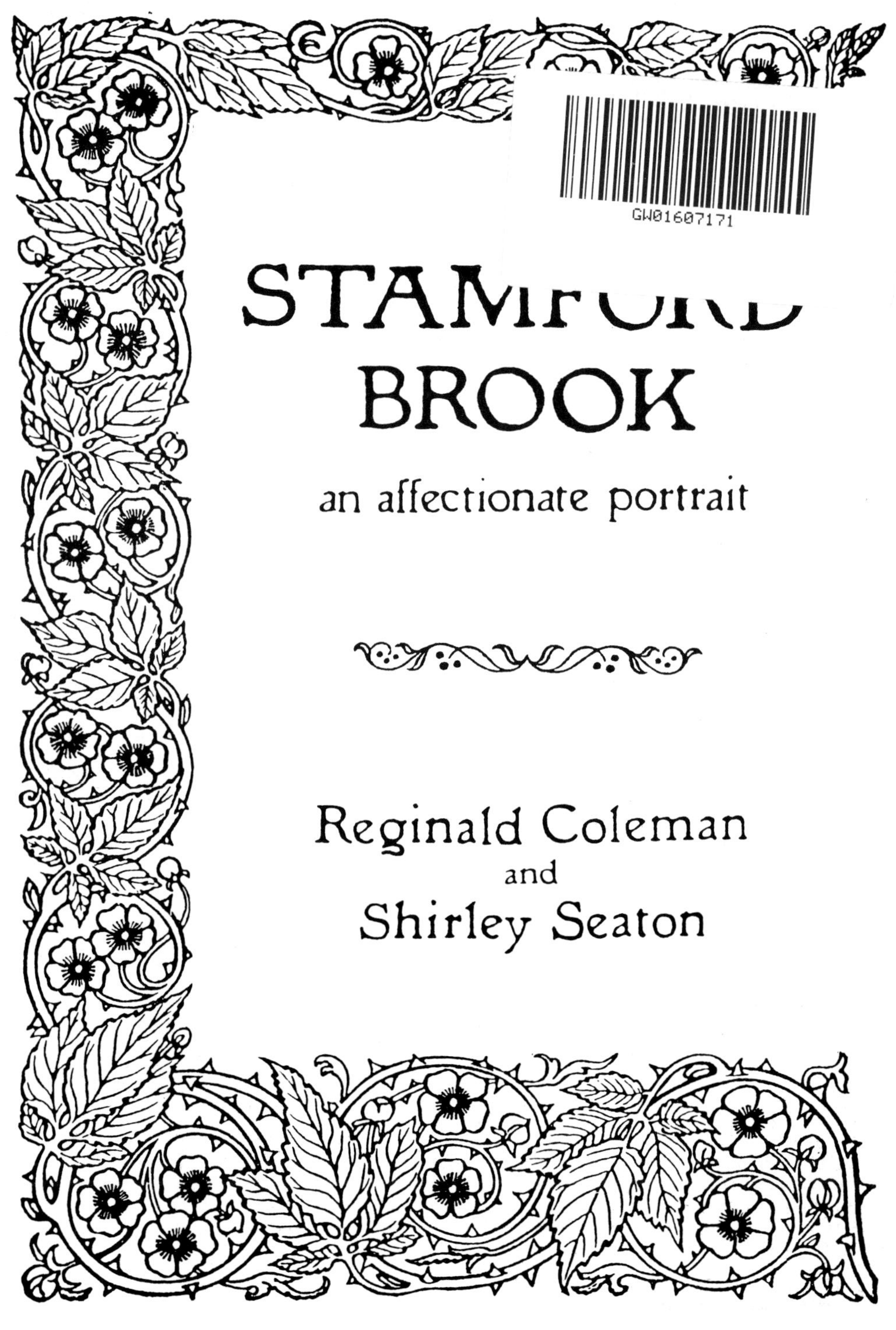

STAMFORD BROOK

an affectionate portrait

Reginald Coleman
and
Shirley Seaton

First published 1992 by Stamford Brook Publications
7 South Side Stamford Brook Common London W6 OXY

ISBN 0 9518896 0 5

Revised edition 1997 Stamford Brook Publications

ISBN 0 9518896 1 3

Designed by Shirley Seaton
Printed by the Russell Press Ltd, Nottingham

ACKNOWLEDGEMENTS

Grateful thanks are due first to Carolyn Hammond, the local history librarian at Chiswick Library for her help and encouragement and for so cheerfully dealing with continual queries during our preparation of the first edition. Thanks too to Hammersmith's local history librarians, particularly Elizabeth Aquilina (now retired). We are indebted to the following for information and help: John Bensusan-Butt, the late Felicity Bergel, David Blair at the Church Commissioners' Records Centre, Gillian Clegg, Pissarro Archivist Kristen Erickson, John Frost, Charlotte Gibbons, John Gillham, Averil Harper Smith, Veronica Manoukian, Sybil Pearce, Joachim Pissarro, Doris Price, Nicholas Reed, the late Wanda Sala, Dr Philip Shorvon, Anne Thorold, and to David Bensusan-Butt, Rhoda Bickerdike and Jack Usher who have died since first publication. Particular thanks to Tom Parker for his drawings of Stamford Brook House and The Brook and to Richard Hanson for his special photography. Finally, our grateful thanks to Malcolm Brown for his helpful comments and to Moira Johnston for her expert editing.

The authors also thank the following organisations and individuals for their kind permission to reproduce photographs or other visual material:
Ashmolean Museum, Oxford 30, 32, 35 (top), 37, 39 (bottom), 41 (bottom), 42; Ian Baker/Connor & Butler Collection: Courtesy *London Railway Record Magazine 51; Brentford & Chiswick Times* 69, Christie's Images 13; Christie's, New York 33, Courtauld Institute of Art (Witt Library) 10, 31; Charlotte Gibbons 56; John Gillham 50, 55 (bottom); Hammersmith & Fulham Archives & local history centre 15 (bottom), 17, 23, 27, 46, 47, 61; Hartswood Tennis Club 63; Hounslow Library Network: Chiswick Local Studies Collection 6, 9, 43, 44, 49, 54, 55; London Metropolitan Archive 57 (bottom); Manchester City Art Galleries 41 (top); Silent Books (back cover); Anne Thorold 13, 38 (bottom); Marjorie Wiles 65; Maps courtesy: Ordnance Survey, Southampton 29; Geographers' A-Z Map Co. Ltd. 67 (bottom). All present-day photographs by Shirley Seaton unless otherwise credited.

The authors also wish to acknowledge permission of A.P. Watt Ltd on behalf of Crystal Hale and Jocelyn Herbert to quote from *The House by the River* by A.P. Herbert.

Front cover:	*Jubilee Fête at Bedford Park, London* by Camille Pissarro, 1897 (private collection)
Back cover:	Daisy design by Lucien Pissarro for Binyon *Dream Come True*, Eragny Press 1905
Title page:	Border designed by Lucien Pissarro from Perrault *Histoire de Peau d'Ane*, Eragny Press 1902

CONTENTS

MAPS

INTRODUCTION TO THE NEW EDITION

The success of the first edition of our '*affectionate portrait*' in 1992 was far beyond our expectations, and a number of people have urged me to reissue the book in a new, expanded form. Sadly, this is done after the death of Reginald Coleman and I would like to dedicate this new edition to him. He died in December 1995, aged 95. His memory and interest in everything and everyone had remained undiminished.

This new edition extends our area north and east of the Green, and includes more about the people and their way of life in 'times past'. There are unsavoury details of the Stamford brook, and I thank Averil Harper-Smith for sharing her research and for leading me to the minute books and maps of the Metropolitan Board of Works with their gruesome tales of mid-nineteenth century sanitation. There are many new illustrations, and in this centenary year of Camille Pissarro's visit, his paintings of Stamford Brook are reproduced in colour, as are paintings by his sons Lucien and Ludovic-Rodo. The updating includes the 1994 boundary changes and new building developments, which continue. The book will, I hope, be easier on the eyes with its new typeface, upgraded from PCW to PC.

The original purpose of this local history remains the same. In the words of the 1992 introduction:

'This book invites you to look at a small, but fascinating, area of London. In Roman Britain it was on the main highway to the west. In the Civil War it may well have been where the Royalists' advance towards London was halted. London's first electric trams ran here. At the end of the nineteenth century it was the subject of several paintings by Camille Pissarro, one of the Impressionist masters, and his son, artist and printer Lucien Pissarro, made his home here for over forty years. He too found themes for his brush in Stamford Brook. Our church was a late arrival and has already gone – also departed, a railway and a station. Lost too is the elusive brook which gave the area its name, and we attempt to trace its streams.

The personal reminiscences of Reginald Coleman, who lived in Stamford Brook for over sixty-five years, and the earlier memories of others such as Sir William Bull (born 1863 – Member of Parliament for Hammersmith and local historian), are interwoven with pictures, photographs and maps, documents and printed material from a variety of sources. One notable 'contributor' is A.P. Herbert (Sir Alan Herbert, MP, writer and humorist) on the subject of the overcrowded District Line in 1920) a phenomenon not unfamiliar to residents of Stamford Brook today.

This is not a comprehensive history – it is more of a scrap book of times past – with perhaps a few serendipities. We are not a village clustered around our church and high street of shops, and housing development has had no overall estate plan. The 'Green' is our central point, a busy meeting place in the early morning for dog owners. It is interesting to conjecture whether there is a sense of community.'

Shirley Seaton   February 1997

Throughout the book Reginald Coleman's reminiscences are printed in *italics*.

STAMFORD BROOK ROAD

and bus to Acton Green

Etching by Ludovic-Rodo Pissarro, 1921 from the watercolour sketch illustrated on page 36. Ludovic-Rodo was a younger brother of Lucien Pissarro. He lived at 3 Blenheim Road at times between 1921-5 (where W.B.Yeats had lived during his childhood)

The same view in 1991
St. Mary's Church, hidden by trees on the far left, has been converted into flats.
The Victorian terrace houses in Stamford Brook Avenue on the right are hidden behind increased foliage. The bus, 88 for many years, became a 94 in 1990

PERSONAL PREFACE by REGINALD COLEMAN, 1991

My father was a builder and in 1923 had bought some plots of land in Stamford Brook Avenue and South Side, which had lain vacant since the developer of the blocks of flat Linkenholt Mansions, Ranelagh Gardens and Hauteville Court Gardens had run into financial problems in 1906, and never completed the original development as planned. My father had also acquired the vacant land on the west of Prebend Gardens, north of the railway arch and where a builder had started work on eight houses at the northern end next to the children's playground in 1908, but further extension was interrupted by the outbreak of the 1914-18 war.

In 1926 I came as a young man with my parents to Leafwood, now No.10, Stamford Brook Avenue, built by my father – adjoining Stamford Brook House. At the end of the rear garden, only a few feet away from the brook itself (already conduited), were the remains of a cottage, and a map showed glass houses to the south (see p.29). I wondered what its history had been.

In 1936 I married Clarice Hall, who had lived in Woodstock Road, Bedford Park, since she was a young girl before the 1914-18 war. So, between us we had sixty to seventy years' varied memories of the area – recollections which friends said they found fascinating, and suggested they should be written down.

Being over eighty years old and inexperienced in historical research, I was somewhat reluctant to embark on such a task on my own, but by great good fortune I happened to mention the idea to my friend and neighbour, Shirley Seaton, who is a researcher by profession, and we decided to combine our efforts.

Charter Day, 18 October 1932
The procession passes along Stamford Brook Avenue as the mayors drive around the boundary of the new Brentford and Chiswick Municipal Borough

A WALK ALONG THE OLD PARISH BOUNDARIES

For the area of Stamford Brook we have taken the Common (sometimes called 'the Green' by local people) as the hub of our wheel, and therefore encompass parts of Chiswick (Borough of Hounslow) and Hammersmith (Borough of Hammersmith and Fulham). See the sketch map inside the front cover, which also shows the 1994 borough boundary changes.

If you start your walk at Young's Corner, you will see the first of the six old parish boundary stones inset flat in the pavement by the Normand garage at the corner of British Grove. Cross the road and the second boundary stone is at pavement level in the Goldhawk Road by the rear door of the Midland Bank. Following the boundary, go northwards along Goldhawk Road and you will notice the date the houses were built (1891) above the front doors. At 388 and 392 look upwards at the birds atop the gables – are they 'goldhawks'? The third boundary stone is on the corner of Stamford Brook Avenue behind the petrol station. The site of the petrol station was previously that of Gothic Cottage (see p.23). Continue along the main road (although the actual boundary runs between the gardens of Goldhawk Road and Stamford Brook Avenue) with Queen Charlotte's Maternity Hospital and Oakbrook on your right, until you reach The Queen of England pub (renamed The Brook in 1996), named after Queen Victoria. Turn left into Stamford Brook Road, on the other side note the initials LGOC by the Owen Conway archway (see p.53), next to what was St. Mary's Church, now a block of flats (see p.59). On your left you pass the former newsagents, run by the Nixsons for many years and from where grandmother Nixson sold her homemade icecream (see p.61), beyond which is a tiny folly, The Grotto, deliciously restored. Continue past the cottages, and between Stamford Brook Villa and The Brook, facing the small green called Stamford Brook Open Space, is the fourth stone, marking the north-east boundary of the parish of Chiswick. The Brook, which has been called 'the prettiest house in London', is where Lucien Pissarro lived for many years (see p.20 & pp.37ff.). The fifth boundary stone is in the wall of 26 Stamford Brook Avenue; and this corner is Lucien Pissarro's viewpoint for his painting of the snow-covered Green (p.10). Follow the old boundary line by taking the path across the Common more or less parallel with Stamford Brook Road. Hammersmith is to your right, Chiswick to your left. The boundary turned right along the old railway track at the rear of Abinger Road's gardens. The last boundary stone is where Stamford Brook Road becomes Bath Road.

The Chiswick/Hammersmith parish boundary was also that dividing Middlesex from the County of London. The original designation by the Post Office of most of Stamford Brook, although in Chiswick, as part of the Hammersmith delivery area, creates a situation in which Hounslow Council is the local authority for houses in Hammersmith, W.6.! Post Office delivery areas bear no relation to parish boundaries.

HOW STAMFORD BROOK GOT ITS NAME

STAMFORD is probably derived from STEANFORDE, from the Saxon 'stean', a stone, and 'ford', the passage across a river. The brook crossed the Roman highway immediately to the west of the site of St.Mary's Church, where it seems likely the Romans laid a bed of gravel in the brook to make a ford for passing traffic. Hence the Saxon name, following the Roman occupation: STANFORD, STANDFORD, and finally STAMFORD. As late as the nineteenth century some documents still refer to 'Standford' or 'Stanford' Brook.

STAMFORD BRIDGE/STANFORD BRIDGE/STANDFORD'S BRIDGE*

A sixteen-foot wide, one arch, brick bridge was built about 1820 by the Grand Junction Water Works at this same point, called Stamford Bridge, which appears to have gone over the main stream of the brook. It is drawn on the 1865 O.S. map. According to Thomas Faulkner (*History of Hammersmith*, 1839), the bridge carried an iron pipe conveying water from Kew to the reservoirs at Paddington, but it seems to have disappeared by the 1880s, presumably with general conduiting. During this period the area was often referred to as 'Stamford Bridge'. It was, however, so called before the building of this bridge. Stukeley in 1722 (see p.22) refers to 'Stanford-bridge', and a 1742 property deed of Stamford Brook House describes the land 'situate at Standford's Bridge'. There is also an intriguing account rendered to the Bishop of London by the owner of Stamford Brook House in 1787 'for repairing or building a bridge....£10 (bridge repairs were the responsibility of the Lord of the Manor).

THE ROMAN ROAD

In 1834, workmen making up the Goldhawk Road found the old Roman causeway about ten feet below the surface, and unearthed various articles including Roman coins and small square tiles.

There were three main Roman roads through London: Ermine Street, Watling Street and 'the Roman Road' (later, the Saxons called it Here Street, and the antiquarian Montagu Sharpe, J.P., writing in 1918 named it Tamesis Street). This was the most important Roman highway to the west, connecting *Londinium* with *Aquae Salis* (Bath). Leaving the City of London at Newgate it followed the line of present-day Oxford Street and the continuing road through Bayswater, Notting Hill Gate, Shepherd's Bush, the Goldhawk Road – where it crossed 'Stanford (Stand-ford) Brook' – Bath Road (appropriately named when it was made up in the nineteenth century), across Acton Common and Back Common, most likely joining the Great Western Road where Chiswick Road still cuts through. Thence it went through Brentford, Hounslow, Staines.

**Not to be confused with the Fulham Stamford Bridge.*

FROM 'SEVEN COTTAGES OR TENEMENTS' TO FOUR HOUSES

Stamford Brook straddles the border of Chiswick and Hammersmith, themselves mere 'hamlets' until the nineteenth century. In the Domesday survey of 1086 it was included in the Manor of Fulham's 1560 acres, belonging to St. Paul's Cathedral, an important Middlesex estate of the Bishop of London. By the sixteenth century Stamford Brook was part of Chiswick's Prebendal Manor Estate, leased out by the Chapter of Westminster until acquired by the Ecclesiastical Commissioners in 1882. From 1783 until 1882 special manor court sessions were held at The Roebuck Inn, Chiswick High Road. The Hammersmith area of Stamford Brook was part of the hamlet or territorial district of Palengwyk (Pallenswicke), which had no manor – later the London Bishoprick Estate. In medieval times the area had been one of mixed farming, animals and crops, the tenants cultivating strips of land in large open fields. By the nineteenth century it was an area of market gardens, orchards and meadowland.

Chiswick rate books in the 1630s show a few inhabitants of Turnham Green assessed separately at Stamford Lane, and by the eighteenth century at Stanford Brook. Hammersmith rate books show one name at Stanford Brook under the Starch Green area in 1795. An early description of property at Stamford Brook is found in the deeds of Stamford Brook House (Copy of Admittance of William Skinner dated 1699) - which also refers to an earlier occupation: 'seven cottages or tenements with the garden orchard and two roods of land to the same belonging situated at Standford Brook ... formerly the land and tenements of Humphrey Robinson, George Whitfield and Widow Harvey...' By 1733 (Admittance of Francis Atkins and Edmund Skinner) this has become: 'two messuages [dwelling houses] with outhouse, garden, orchard and appurtenances thereto belonging... formerly seven cottages or tenements, ...' etc.

At the end of the eighteenth century in the Parish of Chiswick there were four houses in Stanford-brook, 163 in Chiswick and 168 at Turnham-green.

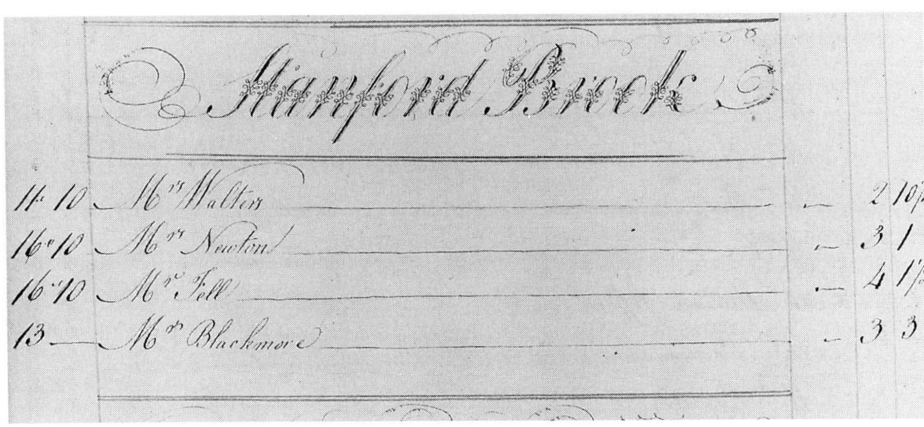

Stanford Brook

11.10	Mrs Walters	2 10½
16.10	Mrs Newton	3 1
16.10	Mrs Fell	4 1½
13	Mrs Blackmore	3 3

Chiswick Church Wardens' Accounts Book

Rates assessments for Stanford Brook, Lady Day, 26 March 1784

Under the clerk's hand-drawn, decorative heading, these are the only entries for Stanford Brook. Rates were 18d in £1. Rateable value of property in L-hand column, amount due in R-hand column

Stamford Brook Green, Sun and Snow **Lucien Pissarro, December 1909 oil**
Stamford Brook Road is on the right, in the distance can be seen the level-crossing keeper's cottage and behind it 62 Bath Road. The houses are those in Gainsborough Road. Prebend Gardens houses were not yet built

Horse trough at the south-east corner of Stamford Brook Common (photo 1990)
Presented in 1905 in commemoration of Queen Victoria's reign, 1837-1901, by the Metropolitan Drinking Fountain & Cattle Trough Association, a charitable organisation still operating today, founded as the Metropolitan Free Drinking Association in 1859 by Samuel Gurney, MP (a nephew of Elizabeth Fry), to eradicate cholera and intemperance by providing a free supply of drinking water. Drinking troughs for dogs, cattle and horses were added later

I remember seeing the Household Cavalry, on their way to Windsor from duty at Buckingham Palace, dismounted around the Common and watering their horses from canvas buckets filled from this trough.

STAMFORD BROOK COMMON

Until the latter half of the nineteenth century and the Bedford Park development, the area known today as Stamford Brook Common was a continuation of Turnham Green Back Common. It is described as such in the Tithe Apportionments map of 1847, and deeds of Stamford Brook House with the Prebendal Manor of Chiswick define the western boundary of the property as 'the brick wall (still there) which is facing on to the Back Common.'

THE BATTLE OF TURNHAM GREEN
Sunday, 13 November 1642

It is a matter for conjecture whether the field of battle of this Civil War encounter extended as far as Stamford Brook. Sir William Bull thought so, asserting: 'The site of the Church (St.Mary's) stands on the rear of the battlefield.'

After the Battle of Brentford, the Royalist forces under Prince Rupert spent the night on Turnham Green Back Common before their encounter with the Parliamentary army, which, reinforced by the trained bands of London, numbered some 24,000 men 'led out in their brightest equipage' under the command of the Earl of Essex.

Contemporary accounts vary as to the ferocity of the battle. One Roundhead source numbers 800 Cavaliers slain, but according to other reports the many hedges in the area hindered any cavalry engagement, and although there was some musket fire, the armies faced each other all day, with no progress made by either side. Some suggested that the armies had kept the Sabbath. When darkness fell the the Cavaliers quietly retreated, 'with no noise of drum beating and with colours furled', across the river to Kingston, and from thence to Reading and Oxford. From London the wives of the Parliamentarians sent cartloads of provisions and wines, and after the retreat of the King's army, they sat on the Green and feasted. Whether or not it was a 'battle', or merely a long-drawn-out skirmish, it was here the King abandoned his march on the capital, so ending his hopes of a quick victory.

Over two hundred years later a Cavalier's spur was found buried in a fork of one of the elm trees in Ravenscourt Park, causing Sir William Bull to ponder: 'Had a gallant Cavalier got through the half mile which divided Charles from Ravenscourt House?'

The 2½ acres of Common Land of the Prebendal Manor of Chiswick, now Stamford Brook Common, was first taken under the wing of a local authority in 1881, when the 'Inclosure Commissioners for England and Wales' under the Metropolitan Commons Acts of 1866 and 1869 gave responsibility for the administration of the land to the Chiswick Improvement Commissioners, known as 'the Board'. This body was the forerunner of the local Parish Council, later to become Brentford & Chiswick Council, and subsequently absorbed into Hounslow Borough Council.

About one eighth of the Common - i.e. that portion north of the present path running east/west nearly parallel with Stamford Brook Road – lay within the Borough of Hammersmith (since the boundary change of 1994 it is Hounslow), and it took many years for Chiswick to carry out any improvements, arguing 'as the Common lies on the borders of the Parish and is used mainly by residents in Hammersmith' Hammersmith Borough Council should contribute to its upkeep.

It remained rough grassland that was often waterlogged, and in 1912 letters from local residents to *The Chiswick Times* complained of the 'deplorable state' of the Common. One man refers to it as a swamp, and mentions that the public seats are pitiful in appearance and that 'one, in particular, is nearly level with the ground, sunk lower one end than the other, and is generally the centre of a large pool of water'.

At last, in 1912, improvement plans were initiated by Chiswick Urban District Council, to include grass tennis courts, croquet lawns, which should be possible to convert later to a bowling green, and an area (the small recreation ground the other side of Prebend Gardens) for the use of women and children only. Cricket and football clubs had for some years been allowed to use the ground for matches, including the local Prebend Football Club, but there were complaints of 'bad language' and rowdyism by footballers on Sundays, and plain clothes police were requested to patrol the area. The 10th Battalion (DCO)/Middx Territorials, whose new headquarters were at Stamford Brook Lodge Drill Hall, trained on the Common on Monday evenings. Strong iron railings and gates replaced the rough wooden posts (see 1909 painting p.10) surrounding the Common, and on 19 June 1913 Stamford Brook Common opened with a full-time keeper on duty. Two croquet lawns had been completed, to be hired at 8d an hour including the croquet set. Six grass tennis courts were opened the following summer. In December 1916 Mrs. Saunders took over the duties of park keeper, when Mr. A.J. Cooper was called up for military service. Sadly, he was killed in 1918, just before the Armistice.

When I arrived in 1926 paths had been laid, as at today, and the croquet lawns had disappeared. The railings had been replaced by upright posts painted black and white, and joined by very heavy cast-iron chains which was quite attractive.

With the outbreak of the war in 1939 all this changed. The tennis courts became vegetable allotments and the cast- iron chains went for scrap. Two longish underground air raid shelters were constructed at the western end of the Common, with the local ARP Post located on the other side of Prebend Gardens where there was a children's playground until recently (see p.64).

At the end of the war the question of housing was a priority of the local authorities, and in the autumn of 1945 it was proposed that a small number of pre-fabricated houses should be erected on the Green.

Many of the local residents felt that common land should not be expropriated for this purpose, particularly as the cost of installing public utility services of water, drains, gas, electricity, etc. for such a small number of pre-fabs was completely uneconomic. A retired house-owner in Pleydell Avenue and I (who had just been demobilised from the Army, and was out of a job), collected a petition of signatures in the neighbourhood against. In the course of this exercise, one elderly house-owner berated me with veiled threats of action on the grounds that my father had told her that the outlook would never be impaired, as the house faced common land.

In the event, our pleas had no effect on the Chiswick officials, but somebody remembered the Hammersmith interest in major issues affecting the Common, and we submitted our petition to that authority. By good fortune Hammersmith supported our objections and the proposal was shelved.

In the years following the war the Common reverted to grassland as we know it now, with iron railings enclosing it. A red shale tennis court was built in the south-eastern corner but it was uneconomic for the Council to collect playing fees and it was subsequently dug up.

In 1989 Hounslow Council built a playground for small children in this area, with colourful climbing ropes, wendy house and slide, with a wood-chip base and enclosed against dogs. The playground at the north-west corner of Prebend Gardens with its concrete base has been demolished as unsafe – gone are the swings, seesaw and slide, in the past much enjoyed by older children. Since 1987 the land has reverted to 'waste'. While various planning applications are considered for residential building on this site, the rubbish accumulates.

* * *

Stamford Brook Green, Snow
Lucien Pissarro, 1927 oil

Painted from the front window of Orovida's top floor flat at 2 Stamford Gardens. Stamford Brook Road is on the right and in the distance the bell tower of St. Michael & All Angels, Bedford Park. The distant tower on the left may be the water tower at Brentford which Sir William Bull said could be seen from Oakbrook, in the Goldhawk Road

THE ELUSIVE BROOK

Various maps dating from the seventeenth century show evidence of three main branches of Stamford brook. The middle branch is that most often shown, but there is no consensus on the number of branches, their names or their courses. The map of 1855 reproduced opposite is one of very few to show all three branches. It is now one of London's lost rivers – a sewer, running completely underground.

The east branch rose north of Wormwood Scrubs and ran between the Scrubs and Old Oak Common, down along the Acton/Hammersmith parish boundary to Askew and Paddenswick roads, to join the main stream east of Ravenscourt Park.

The middle, main, branch (often called Stamford brook west branch), followed a winding course from the north down Horn Lane, Acton, across the High Street at the foot of Acton Hill,* flowing south-east through Stamford Brook Fields to cross Stamford Brook Road (the old Roman road) west of St. Mary's Vicarage, thence along the eastern side of The Brook cottage, behind Stamford Brook House, turning sharply east by the Ranelagh Gardens flats to cross Goldhawk Road south of Oakbrook. It then fed the moat around the mansion (destroyed by bombs in 1941) in what is now Ravenscourt Park. This branch is clearly shown on the Rocque map of 1746 (reproduced p.67). It took much of Acton's drainage – and continues to do so. The 'stone ford' where it crossed the Roman highway gives the area its name..

The third, west branch, rose on Hanger Hill, where it was called 'the boundary brook' (being the boundary between Acton and Ealing parishes). It ran down the side of Bollo Lane (on the boundary between Ealing/Acton – later Chiswick/Acton), and here it was called Bollo Brook (although it has also been identified as Mill Hill Brook). Turning eastward alongside Acton Green/Turnham Green Back Common it then seems to have run north of the Bath Road, with a ditch also running along south of the road, to join with the the middle branch west of Ravenscourt Park. Part of this stream was diverted at Acton Green to run south to form the ornamental lake in the grounds of Chiswick House. The turnpike map shows these two routes as do early Ordnance Surveys.

All the streams converged east of Ravenscourt Park and ran south, crossing King Street near the municipal Civic Centre into what was known as The Creek. Here Stamford brook was tidal, and flowed into the Thames.

The Creek was once an area of great activity with barges from the river loading and unloading at the wharves on either side. I remember during the period 1915-20, as a pupil at Latymer Upper School, and at that time living at Bishops Park, Fulham, walking along the Mall from under Hammersmith Bridge and as I crossed the Creek by a humped wooden bridge, looking at the sailing barges moored there. It was a crowded area of small, rather poor houses, and sometimes called Little Wapping.

The Creek was filled in in 1936, and today is covered by Furnivall Gardens and across the motorway by the large blocks of flats Riverside and Aspen Gardens.

*The road was over four metres lower than the modern road, the hill steep, and waggoners were warned at the top of the hill of the water splash, which as late as 1899 was a major obstacle.

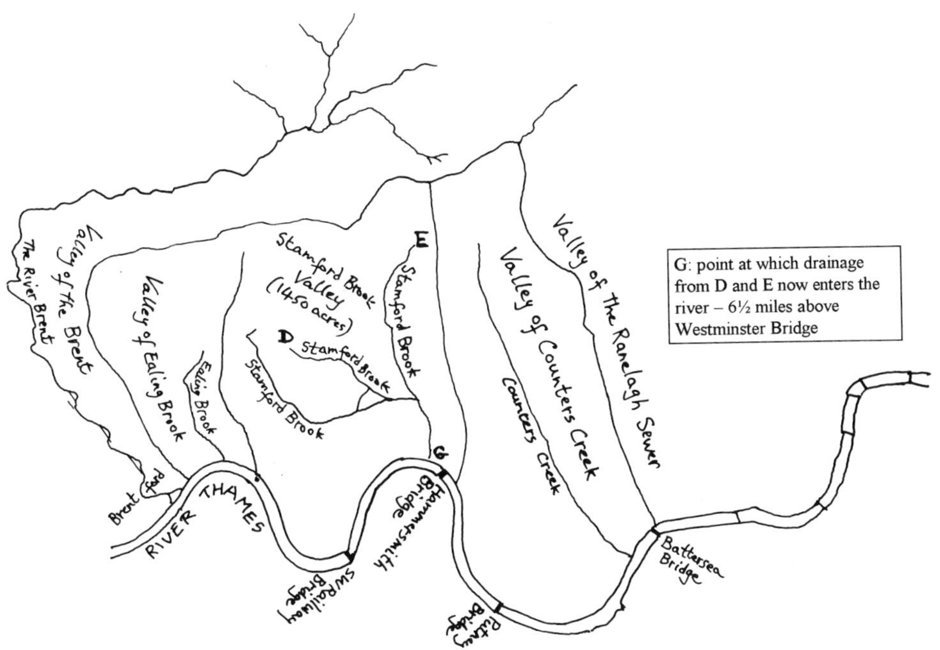

The natural valleys to the north-west of the Thames, based on a map prepared by Henry Law, civil engineer, in 1855 for the Metropolitan Commissioners for Sewers during consultation for Joseph Bazalgette's scheme for main drainage. One of the few maps to show all three branches of Stamford brook

The Creek, Hammersmith, with moored barges 1929

There is, however, evidence to suggest that the middle branch of the Stamford brook divided at the point where it turned east towards Ravenscourt Park, a stream continuing south along the parish boundary line. The Geological Survey 6" map 1935/6 surprisingly shows no watercourse, visible or concealed, as entering The Creek, but it does show a watercourse connected with the brook entering a smaller creek (now filled in) opposite the north eastern tip of Chiswick Eyot, after running south along the boundary between Hammersmith and Chiswick. This stream also seems indicated on Wyld's map of 1870. That there was such a stream seems not unlikely; ancient ecclesiastical manor boundaries were often delineated by rivers, as are London borough boundaries today.

With the increase in population and house building in the nineteenth century, the streams of Stamford brook, pure and clear as they flowed through the rural countryside, had become very polluted. A writer in 1889 (Kemp's *West London Sketcher*) lamented: 'We well remember catching the agile but thoughtlessly voracious tittlebat in the little brook which formerly ran where Bedford Park now stands, but where is the angler now-a-days who could perform as much?' No doubt referring to Stamford brook east branch, in 1899 a pedestrian making his way up Old Oak Common Lane had to 'run the gauntlet (to one's nose) of this disgraceful open sewer which was once a purling crystal brooklet'.It was not culverted here until 1920.

By the middle of the century the accumulation of sewage in open ditches and the increase in frequency and intensity of cholera and typhus epidemics, was forcing the government to take action regarding entire reconstruction of the main drainage of the London area. Stamford brook had become a sewer, part culverted but part still open – stagnant and foul smelling, and condemned by surveyors for the Metropolitan Commission for Sewers, who in 1849 were sickened by the stench from the ditch where men were removing the foul deposit of years, naming it as possibly the source of cholera and typhus in the nearby cottages. This was off the Uxbridge Road, where Stamford brook east branch crossed. In the delay for any permanent remedy, ditches were cleaned out – but locally the filth was not carted away, being cast upon the banks and covered with fresh ground lime, a method not as effective as intended against the noxious odours. Letters and petitions from the residents from Stamford Brook to Ravenscourt, bordering this stagnant ditch, continually pleaded with the Metropolitan Board of Works to culvert the brook. Petitions with up to 49 signatures, usually in the hot summer months when residents were forced to keep the windows shut, repeatedly got the same reply for over fifteen years, even when reinforced by a letter from the Medical Officer for Health, a doctor with a practice in the Goldhawk Road. The Commissioners' engineer, the renowned Joseph Bazalgette, advised the Board to take no action, other than to have it cleansed, until deciding on his overall scheme for the reconstruction of London's main drainage.This area of the Stamford brook was at last diverted and culverted in 1865-6.

The main brick sewer was five foot in internal diameter. Sir William Bull (see p.26) wrote in 1929: 'You can now, if you get permission, wade up the old river underground, as far as Acton'. In 1990 Thames Water said 'Yes, you can. But it's rather expensive and the stink is terrible!'

RIVULETS OFF THE MAIN STREAMS

The unmapped rivulets off the main streams have caused many problems in the area, when workmen have struck unsuspected water. In the 1950s during construction of the extension to the Royal Masonic Hospital, it was necessary to lay a special concrete screen base, since the brook ran beneath the site.

When the petrol station (on the site of the old Victorian house called Gothic Cottage at the junction of Goldhawk Road and Stamford Brook Avenue) was being built, I recall passing the site on my way to the station when the workmen were excavating a deep space for one of the large container tanks. A crowd of men were gazing with amazement at water slowly filling the bottom of the deep pit. I said to the foreman, 'I see you've struck part of the brook!', of which he was ignorant, since there was nothing on their plans, as the main stream, as mentioned, turned eastward behind Ranelagh Gardens. In the event, the company had to make a concrete platform.

Mr. L. Chapman, of W. Chapman & Sons, builders, remembered: 'Some time about 1920, before the houses on the west side of Emlyn Road were built, a shallow stream ran parallel to the railway line and the local lads (I was one of them) used to fish for tiddlers. It was always referred to as "the brook".'

Earlier, Maurice Adams, one of the architects of Bedford Park 'Garden City', notes along the eastern border of his 1896 plan: 'By the side of Stamford brook willow trees furnished a rural walk towards Acton'. A romantic image, rather different from MP Sir William Bull's childhood memories of the 1870s when he carried his little sister 'on dark winter nights over the mud of the morass which always surrounded the level crossing on the eastern side'.

Part of the culvert of the Stamford brook found under the premises of Messrs Selden & Son, 180 King St., Hammersmith.
A.O.Collard, June 1910

Drawing by Tom Parker, 1991

STAMFORD BROOK HOUSE

An attractive Georgian house facing onto Stamford Brook Common at the east end, it was the first house of any size to be built in our area. Until 1904 Stamford Brook House was copyhold property, held of the Prebend Manor of Chiswick.

The present house was built by Thomas Patterson, most likely about 1743. It remained copyhold of the Patterson family until 1817, and the following year 'brewhouse' was added to the description, which reads: 'messuage or tenement brewhouse coachhouse stables and premises'. In 1823 the copyhold was purchased by George Scott, of Ravenscourt, increasing to the west his already large estate.

From 1795 until the 1860s the house was the residence of the Frere family, originally sugar plantation owners in the Barbados. Applewhaite Frere, who died in 1830, is buried at St. Paul's, Hammersmith, where he is commemorated in a marble memorial tablet on the west wall. He was succeeded by his elder son, John Frere, magistrate for the County of Middlesex, who lived at Stamford Brook House with his footman, housekeeper, cook and housemaid. He acquired two houses in Williams Terrace (the Georgian terrace, which can still be seen at the start of Chiswick High Road, south side) and land which included pasture and a paddock between Stamford Lane and the New Road, and three fields with over six acres of meadowland south of Stamford Brook Common. John was succeeded in July 1864 by his younger brother, Tobias, who was married to Cassandra, daughter of Thomas Atwood, Chief Justice of the Bahama Islands. Tobias outlived his brother by little over a year. They are both buried in St. Mary's Parish Church, Acton.

At the turn of the century Stamford Brook House was occupied by Mr. and Mrs. Macgregor. Pioneers in social work, they were two of the founders of the Hampshire House Trust and Club, Hammersmith, a working men's social and educational club, with activities including exhibitions and athletics as well as classes. In 1909, Ellen McGregor started one of London's first infant welfare centres in a room in Ravenscourt Park. Archibald Grey Macgregor (died 1909) was art master at the Crystal Palace School of Art where Esther, wife of Lucien Pissarro, had been a student before her marriage. The Pissarros at The Brook, and the Macgregors remained close friends. Ellen Macgregor survived her husband for many years, dying in 1951 aged 93. Their son, John Macgregor, architect and conservationist, was responsible for the major studio conversion at The Brook in 1935.

Mrs. Macgregor was an interesting character. At the time of the Boer war she raised money in support of the Boer women and children and, my father told me, she was a suffragette. In her latter years, Mrs. Macgregor used to have tea parties in the garden (next to where I lived) with elderly lady guests still dressed in rather Edwardian costume – large brimmed hats and carrying parasols – reminiscent of Queen Alexandra.

STAMFORD BROOK LODGE & DRILL HALL

Built probably in the 1830s with entrance drive and large front garden, where the huge Drill Hall was built in 1911 after it was bought by the Middlesex Regiment, becoming the Headquarters of 10th Battalion (DCO). The house was demolished in the 1970s and the drill hall in 1987. It is now the site of Stamford Brook Avenue Nursing Home and Park Mansions flats.

THE PARAKEETS

Over thirty years ago ring-necked parakeets took up residence in the grounds of Chiswick House, Ravenscourt Park and Stamford Brook House. At Stamford Brook House Mrs. Bergel used to feed about ten birds every day until she moved in 1988. The birds have withstood harsh winters, but there are fewer now, and in summer just before dusk they swoop over this area in groups, distinguishable by their loud, raucous call and their long tails. The vivid green plumage looks dark in the twilight. Brought originally from India, these birds escaped from captivity, and were first noted in London at the end of the last century.

In the 1970s a BBC producer who lived in Ranelagh Gardens arranged for a team from Nationwide *to film these birds. I rose at 5.30 a.m. to greet the crew, and cameras etc. were all in place in the adjacent garden by 7 a.m. They waited (drinking many cups of coffee) until 10.30, but not a bird arrived – the first day for over a month we hadn't seen them.*

Drawing by Tom Parker 1991

THE BROOK

Nikolaus Pevsner *The Buildings of England: London* 1952 describes The Brook as 'a rare detached Georgian cottage'. Set back from Stamford Brook Road, it nestles beyond the willow tree and Stamford Brook 'Open Space', its eastern wall marking Chiswick's boundary with Hammersmith and also the course of Stamford brook. In 1976 a blue plaque was placed on the house commemorating the residence there of Lucien Pissarro, painter, printer and wood engraver. A hand-painted name plate proclaiming 'Ancient Lights' is fixed alongside, and seems likely to have been put up by Esther Pissarro after a neighbourly dispute.

Until 1878 The Brook was copyhold property held of the Prebend Manor of Chiswick. With the house went land stretching up to what is now Stamford Brook Avenue.

The main house is late seventeenth century, timber framed. The earliest deed dated 1767 describes it as 'all that one Cottage or Tenement formerly divided into two Messuages with 24 perches of land' previously in the possession of Henry Thompson of Stamford Brook, Chiswick, and Jane, his wife '...now in the possession or occupation of William Blackmore'.

William Blackmore bricked over the house, as it is now. He lined the walls with newspapers of the period (found some years ago during replastering), which were covered with fishing-net on a painted canvas, giving the effect of a lattice-patterned wallpaper. William (died 1799), his wife Ann and their two daughters Ann and Susannah (who lived to the age of 92) are buried at St. Nicholas' Parish Church, Chiswick, where they are commemorated by a headstone, lying flat next to William Hogarth's tomb. The Blackmores seem to have had large farming interests in Hertfordshire and Kent. William Henry Blackmore (died 1860) was a London cotton merchant.

Generations of Blackmores lived at The Brook until it was purchased in 1878 by Thomas Hussey, a builder who was also a brickmaker on Stamford Brook Fields, nearly opposite. By 1881 Hussey had built the row of five 4-storey terraced houses (1-5 Stamford Gardens - now 28-20 Stamford Brook Avenue), on the western end of The Brook land, and three of them were already occupied. It is believed he planned to build more flats on the site of The Brook, but, luckily for us because he lost the action brought by the Chiswick Local Board in 1890 regarding the nuisance and smells of burning bricks, he was forced to curtail his building plans.

In 1901 Thomas Hussey let the house to Lucien Pissarro (see p.37), imposing an undertaking to carry out immediate repairs. By then the house and garden were in a ruinous state – there were no drains and water had to be pumped from a well in the garden. There were gaps in the roof, and in an upstairs room water dripped from the ceiling into a rusty tin bath. His father, Camille Pissarro, loaned them the money, and after months of repairs and conversions, turning the stables into a studio and the scullery and greenhouse into their printing-room, they moved there in April 1902, buying the property when it was put up for sale in 1919, after Hussey had died. It was Lucien's wife, Esther, who had first fallen in love with the cottage, and she continued to lavish improvements on it and the garden throughout her life. The gnarled apple and pear trees and an old vine attracted Lucien's artist's eye, and he was to paint The Brook garden several times. Esther became a keen gardener and corresponded with Monet, exchanging views on gardens, at one time trying to find a rake to Monet's specifications to clean out his lily pond at Giverny.

Lucien died while living at Fishpond, near Charmouth, Dorset, during the Second World War. After Esther died in 1951 their ashes were scattered in their beloved garden.

Esther had hoped to turn The Brook into a Pissarro museum, but it was not large enough nor suitable.

Lucien's paintings and sketch books, along with their diaries and a vast amount of correspondence and other ephemera, were left to the Ashmolean Museum, Oxford, where, thanks to a generous Getty Foundation grant, there is a catalogued and accessible Pissarro archive.

Members of the family still live at The Brook.

GOLDHAWK ROAD

When William Stukeley, the antiquarian, attempted to follow the old Roman highway to London in 1722 he commented:

> Now between Staines and London it is the common road till you come to Turnham green: there the present road through Hammersmith and Kensington leaves it; for it passes more northward upon the common, where to a discerning eye the trace of it is manifest; then it goes over a little brook called from it Stanford-bridge, and comes into the Acton road at a common... I rode the broken part of it between Acton road and Turnham green: it is still a narrow straight way, keeping its original direction, but full of dangerous sloughs, being a clayey soil and never repaired.

The main routes from London to the west had become the North Highway (the Uxbridge Road) and the Great Western (the road through Hammersmith, Chiswick, Brentford). The Roman road from Shepherd's Bush had become Gold Lock Lane, then Goldhawke Road, and the connection with the Great Western was by Stamford Brook Lane at the junction we know as Young's Corner. With the modernising of the stretch between Askew Road to King Street in the 1830s – originally called Oxford Street Road or the New Road, and later known as Goldhawk Road for the whole length – the narrow Stamford Brook Lane approach was replaced. Stamford Brook Lane became Stamford Brook Avenue, and its junction with the Goldhawk Road was completely closed to road traffic in 1971.

Houses soon lined the new road towards Young's Corner (see p.45). Sir William Bull, MP, provided a vivid description of the road as it was in 1878, when he came as a boy to live at Starch Green:

> My old friend, the late well-known journalist, George Augustus Sala (1828-1896), once described the Goldhawk Road as 'the prettiest road out of London' and it really was when I first remember it, with its charming little villas coyly hidden behind low walls and shrubs and trees of all kinds. There was no curbing on the paths from the Queen of England to Young's Corner but pleasant patches of grass beside raised gravel paths. There was a farmhouse and buildings opposite Young's Corner.* Of course there were no trams and the Newman horse busses were the only method of getting direct to Oxford Street and the City. Starch Green pond† was unenclosed and often in hot weather the drivers of heavy wagons would direct their horses through the pond for a drink or to cool their heels. Askew (then Starch Green Road) was a pretty lane with few houses on it, and west of this was all fields. The chief industries were the brick fields of Acton and the laundries of Starch Green. The back of St. Mary's was all fields; Rylett Road was built, but nothing beyond to the west or north.

* (illustration p.44)
† now Starch Green Open Space

Stamford Brook corner, Goldhawk Road, c.1902
Looking west, The Queen of England public house (rebuilt 1926) is on the right, corner shops on the left-hand bend are a bootmaker, an artists' materials dealer, also a stationer-newsagent and tobacconist, a confectioner, a grocer and a laundry. The 143 tram is en route from Kew Bridge to Shepherd's Bush

Gothic Cottage, 372 Goldhawk Road in 1956
One of the first houses to be built on the New Road, at the junction with Stamford Brook Avenue, it was the home of the Murcott family for many years. Seen here shortly before it was demolished. It is now the site of the Fina petrol station

NINETEENTH CENTURY DEVELOPMENT
STAMFORD BROOK ROAD

The Queen of England, on the bend of the Goldhawk Road as it sweeps south (The Brook pub restaurant since 1996), was named after the young Queen Victoria who ascended the throne in 1837. The row of cottages to the west of the pub was built c.1837, in what is now Stamford Brook Road. Nikolaus Pevsner (*The Buildings of England*: *London* 1952) calls them: 'semi-detached well-mannered cottages, interrupted by number 15, The Grotto, a tiny folly, very random rubble'. This delightful gingerbread house was built by James Cubitt (who is said to be related to the famous Cubitt building brothers) in 1838. The cottages to the west were named: Myrtle, Ivy Lodge, Laburnham, Laurel (4-1, now 17-23 Stamford Brook Road). Stamford Brook Villa (25 Stamford Brook Road), which dates from the same period, is on the site of an earlier candle factory.

STAMFORD BROOK FIELDS

These consisted of about 50 acres of meadowland stretching north from Stamford Brook Common, with a cottage and a sheephouse, originally belonging to the Bishop of London and later part of the London Bishoprick Estates. Stamford Brook Fields were so called because they were crossed by the main branch of Stamford brook meandering its way from Acton. In the parish of Hammersmith except for an odd triangle of land, now 65 and 67 Emlyn Road, it was formerly a corner of Stamford Brook grounds, a 'detached' part of Ealing, which became Chiswick from 1878, then Hounslow, and since the 1994 boundary changes it too is in Hammersmith. No.69 Emlyn Road is built over the Stamford brook sewer.

The fields were leased in 1799 to Thomas Essex (succeeded by his son John), a large landowner and farmer in Acton (Cowper-Essex Estate), the freehold remaining with the Bishop of London. In 1876 they were leased to Thomas Hussey for brickmaking, and for over ten years until 1890 he made a large quantity of bricks, many being used to build the houses of Bedford Park. Brickmaking was a smelly business, much disliked by those who lived nearby. Hussey collected refuse from all over London which he burnt and sifted to obtain ash and cinders. These were mixed with clay (brickearth) to make the bricks and fired in a clamp or a kiln over a three-month period, between June and September. In 1889 Hussey used a huge clamp about 200 yards long and 20 yards wide, making a total of seven million bricks, more than in any other year.

Following complaints from residents of Bedford Park of nauseous smells from the brick burning (a complaint not unfamiliar in connection with the Acton brickfields) a High Court action was taken against Hussey by the Chiswick Local Board in 1890. It was (unusually) successful. Hussey was forced to cease brickmaking and to pay the Court costs. Hussey also had building agreements north and south of Stamford Brook Common and east of the Common on land belonging to The Brook, which he had purchased in 1878. In Stamford Brook Road he completed only four houses, numbers 32-38, which were built with his bricks.

The court case ruined him, and by 1897 he was attempting to pay off his creditors and to obtain a release from his building agreements.

The developer who succeeded Hussey south of Stamford Brook Common was J.A. Gill Knight, of Walham Green. His equivalent to the north was William George Chapman of Rylett Road, whilst the developer of the Young's Corner area, which included Prebend Gardens south of the railway viaduct, was John Carter of Dalling Road. Both these men, with local interest, were not purely speculators like Hussey and Gill Knight.

The Grotto, Stamford Brook Road
A tiny folly built with clinker and reject bricks from the brickfields by James Cubitt in 1838. Restored by architect Judith Bottomley c.1970.

Two other follies were built about 1890 in Rylett Road (see p.57). These are more military in style than the Grotto gingerbread house

Letter from Wm.Holditch Stevens, architect, of 21 Ashchurch Grove, Shepherd's Bush, to the Ecclesiastical Commissioners, 31 May 1883:

Gentlemen

Apropos of the proposal to make up the Stamford Brook Road might I be permitted as a resident in the immediate vicinity to put in a plea for the ancient elm trees (of such magnificent growth) which if the road be widened at its eastern end may lead to their destruction. These natural beauties now present a most rural aspect to the eye on approaching the Common from Goldhawke Road. and I am sure the wish of all the residents must be that such may be spared....

Stamford Brook Road was made up and widened in 1884.
The trees survived until 1913 (see illustrations pp.10 and.27).

The Right Hon. Sir William Bull, lst Bt

(1863-1931)

Member of Parliament for Hammersmith from 1900 to 1929. A colourful personality and outspoken in the House, he was ordered out in 1912 for disorderly conduct after calling Asquith 'traitor' during the debate on Irish Home Rule. He worked tirelessly for numerous local organisations and was the first person to be made a Freeman of the Borough of Hammersmith. He was a solicitor, a partner in the family law firm of Bull & Bull. In 1904 he married Lilian, daughter of Gabriel (died 1888) and Cecile Brandon of Oakbrook, the large Victorian Gothic house, still there in Goldhawk Road (see p.56).

I remember seeing him with the other VIPs at Latymer Upper School around 1920, of which he was a Governor. One item in his political career which fascinated me was that in the 1920s he was Chairman of the Channel Tunnel Committee and a strong advocate of the building of the tunnel.

He campaigned for a 'green girdle' to be preserved around London (1901), for parliamentary reform, for votes for women, and as early as 1919 he was advocating more tube trains to solve the traffic problem.

From the age of fourteen, he lived in Percy Road, Starch Green, and became a member of St. Mary's congregation in 1881 as a young man, involved in the running of the Mission Sunday School and Boys Club, starting a weekly savings bank for the parents, and on the Building Committee for the new church. Later he lived in Westcroft Square and at The Meadows in the Uxbridge Road. He wrote histories of St. Mary's, Stamford Brook (in a series of articles for the church magazine in 1929), St. Peter's, Hammersmith, and the Hammersmith Congregational Church.

Right*:* **St. Mary's Church c.1898**

After realignment of Stamford Brook Road and planting of plane trees (see p.25). Two of the four ancient elm trees can be seen on the left and Stamford Brook Villa is on the right. The Vicarage is not yet built.

A single, rather cracked-sounding bell called worshippers on Sundays, and Lucien Pissarro who from 1902 lived at The Brook, virtually opposite, said it tolled 'damn, damn, damn!'

CHURCHES

As merely a small group of cottages straddling the border of the parishes of Chiswick and Hammersmith, Stamford Brook had no church of its own until the late nineteenth century, when the house building boom and increasing population – and a church-going Victorian society – had led to the building of a number of churches in the area. St. Peter's, Hammersmith, was completed earlier, in 1829, Christ Church, Turnham Green in 1843, and nearby in Bedford Park St. Michael & All Angels opened in 1880. Next in line was St. Mary's, Stamford Brook.

ST. MARY'S

St. Mary's had started in 1877 as a small 'iron' (ie corrugated iron) church which became the church hall, behind the site of the brick-built structure there today. In November 1881 the first vicar, Mr. Muspratt, was succeeded by the charismatic preacher the Revd W.E. Freeman Greene. Sir William Bull remembered:

> The Revd W.E. Freeman Greene caused quite a sensation in the neighbourhood when he arrived amongst us in November 1881. He was a born preacher with a singularly handsome head and a pleasant voice. Passionately in earnest, he soon filled the little church to overflowing - indeed, in that first summertime of 1882, people sat on rush bottomed chairs, forms and campstools, on the grass around the doors and windows (which were all opened wide for the purpose) in the hope that they might take part in the service and, above all, hear his sermons - which I do not mind confessing we boys found intolerably long. We often did not leave the church until five or sometimes fifteen and twenty minutes past one. People in those days seemed to like a forty minutes' address.

When Freeman Greene arrived in 1881 the congregation had already outgrown its basic 'iron' church. Money was raised by the usual bazaars, concerts, etc., and the foundation stone for the brick-built St. Mary's – architect Charles Gladman – was laid on 23 August 1886. The ceremony was performed by HRH The Duchess of Teck, who was a cousin of Queen Victoria, and mother of the future Queen Mary, consort of King George V. Sir William Bull says he slipped a penny wrapped round with one of his visiting cards under the stone just before it was lowered into place. Thick fog enveloped Stamford Brook when the church was consecrated on the last day of the year.

The Vicarage was originally planned to be built behind the church, but the architect Frederick W.Peel persuaded Mr Freeman Greene that the church would cut out his light and that a much better site would be facing the church and Stamford Brook Road, away from the noise and smell of the London General Omnibus Company (see p.53). Months and years passed as the site was acquired, and building remained at a standstill while Mr Freeman Greene persuaded the Church Commissioners to foot the bill for his increasingly splendid Vicarage. It took fourteen years before it was completed in 1900 – too late to be enjoyed by Mr. Freeman Greene who had died the previous year. He was succeeded by the Revd Charles Neil, a prolific writer of theological pamphlets, who retired in 1916 aged 90!

* * *

Sir William Bull recalled: 'I have very pleasant recollections of the congregation, which after Church, used to indulge in a kind of Sunday Parade across the Common as far as the level crossing and back again to the Starch Green Pond – now alas! filled up.'

SEVENTH DAY ADVENTIST CHURCH

A similar parade takes place on sunny Saturdays a hundred years later. The congregation is overwhelmingly black, and small boys wearing suits and bow ties like their fathers, girls in frilly dresses and women in smart hats, play and promenade on the Common after their service at the Seventh Day Adventist Church on Stamford Brook Road, west of Prebend Gardens.

The Church has been here since 1916. Originally a wooden structure like a Scout hut with a separate brick-built hall at the rear, after it was destroyed by fire in 1971 it was rebuilt as a single brick building, opening in December 1974.

Mrs. Enid Tolman has been a member of the church since 1950. She says there were then about seventy white members, but since 1953 the West Indian membership has increased annually, due to the fact that Seventh Day Adventists are the largest Protestant denomination in the West Indies. The membership now of 400 is mostly from the Caribbean, and she herself is the only white member. Seven other churches have started from this one.

* * *

By the 1970s the congregation at the Anglican St. Mary's had severely dwindled. The church closed in 1984 and has been converted into flats (see p.59).

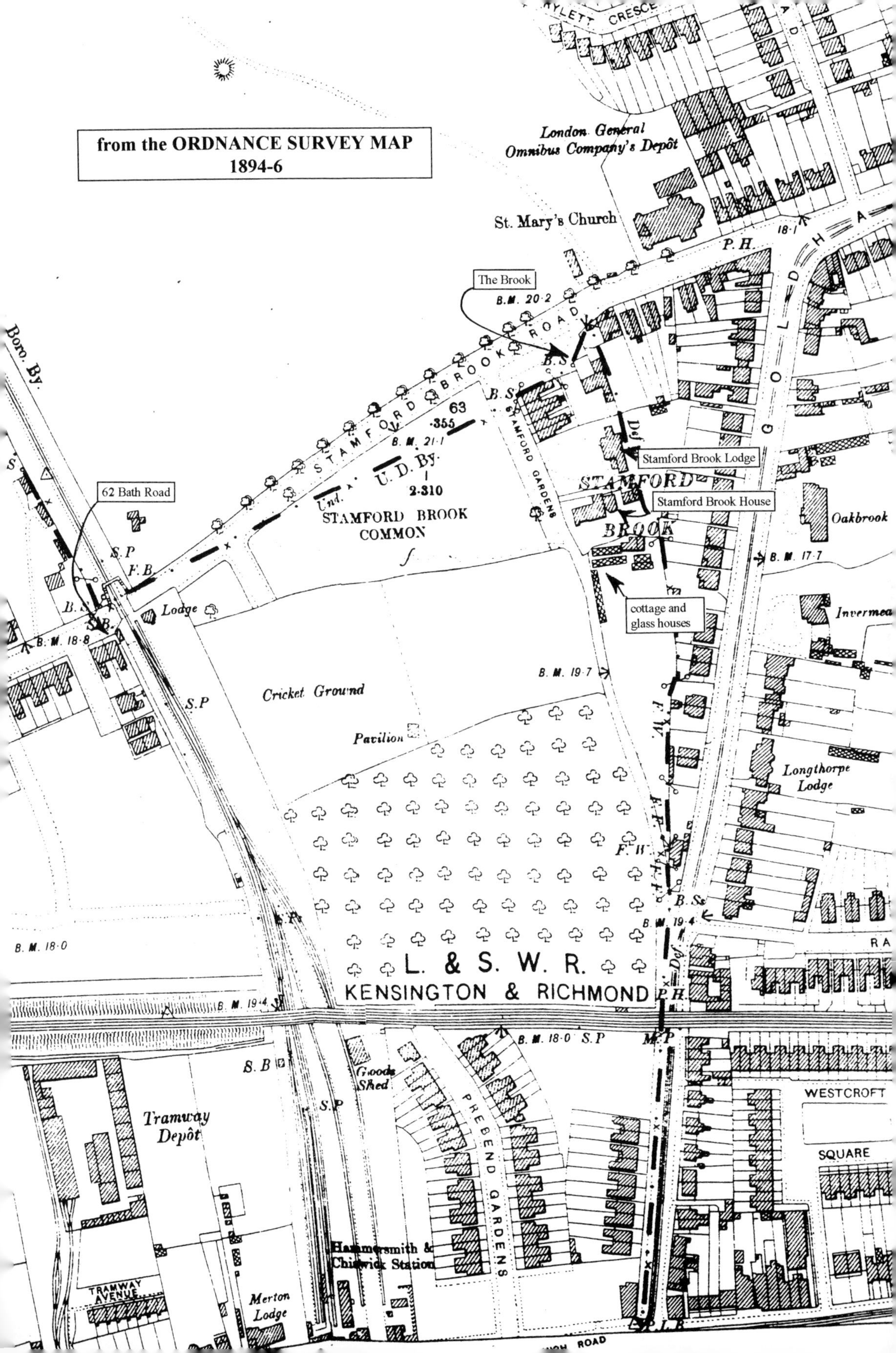

**from the ORDNANCE SURVEY MAP
1894-6**

The Brook

62 Bath Road

Stamford Brook Lodge

Stamford Brook House

cottage and glass houses

London General Omnibus Company's Depôt

St. Mary's Church

STAMFORD BROOK ROAD

STAMFORD GARDENS

STAMFORD BROOK COMMON

STAMFORD BROOK

U. D. By.

Boro. By.

Lodge

Cricket Ground

Pavilion

Oakbrook

Invermead

Longthorpe Lodge

OLD HA...

L. & S. W. R.
KENSINGTON & RICHMOND

Tramway Depôt

Goods Shed

PREBEND GARDENS

WESTCROFT SQUARE

Hammersmith & Chiswick Station

TRAMWAY AVENUE

Merton Lodge

B. M. 20·2

B. M. 21·1

B. M. 18·8

B. M. 17·7

B. M. 19·7

B. M. 19·4

B. M. 18·0

B. M. 18·1

PAINTINGS OF STAMFORD BROOK BY CAMILLE PISSARRO

The great French Impressionist painter, Camille Pissarro (1830-1903), spent his last visit to England at Bedford Park. His son, Lucien, had suffered two strokes, becoming partially paralysed, shortly after the move to 62 Bath Road in April 1897. Camille rushed over from his home at Eragny, north west of Paris, and stayed from 7 May until 19 July while Lucien made a gradual recovery. During these two months he painted seven views, all from the house, front and back, where he set up his easel on the flat roof. He was here at a most propitious time, capturing our area in its final years before house building obscured its rural aspect, and 22 June was the Diamond Jubilee of Queen Victoria, a public holiday with local celebrations taking place over several weeks.

At the end of May he wrote '*je vais me mettre au travail, j'ai ici quelques motifs à faire fort jolis*'. And in mid-June, writing to his friend, the art-dealer Paul Durand-Ruel '...I am hard at work and the sun is really so rare here that I dare not leave my neighbourhood, which is so far from the centre...' The paintings were much admired when he showed them to his friend, the Belgian poet Emile Verhaeren, in Paris on his way home. Although they have been entitled 'Bedford Park', apart from the scene showing 62 Bath Road, they are all of Stamford Brook.

Felix (Camille Pissarro's third son, who died of tuberculosis in November 1897), Lucien and Camille Pissarro on the balcony at the rear of 62 Bath Road.
The railway is below them on the left. Note the signal which appears in Pissarro's painting of *The Train* (see p.35). This is also the viewpoint for his paintings of the cricket matches and the Jubilee fête

Cricket Match at Bedford Park **Camille Pissarro, 1897 oil**

THE CRICKET GROUND

The last quarter of the nineteenth century saw the peak years of the famous cricketer, W.G.Grace, and interest in the game increased with the formation of countless small clubs all over the country. In 1887 meadowland south of what is today South Side was taken over as a cricket ground (see map p.29) for the Broadway Cricket Club, Hammersmith. During the 1897 season Stamford Brook was the home ground for two clubs: Hammersmith, running two teams, and West End Hammersmith, and on most Saturdays there were two cricket matches. Both the clubs had successful seasons, with several centuries scored. Perhaps Pissarro witnessed the amazing boundary in the game on 22 May when a player, as reported in the *West London Observer*, hit a ball into Mr. Broad's garden – Stamford Brook Lodge!

Cricket on the Stamford Brook ground was twice painted by Camille Pissarro. He was fascinated by this English sport, which he had painted at Hampton Court Green on a previous visit. The additional tent which has been erected for the game in the above painting, and the large number of spectators, make it likely to be the match to celebrate the Jubilee played on 29 June at 12 o'clock between Hammersmith and Shepherds Bush Police and Tradesmen, followed at 5.30 by comical sports and dancing. The whereabouts of this painting is unknown. The other painting, *Cricket at Bedford Park*, which was exhibited at the Musée d'Orsay, Paris in 1994-5, is in the Mahmoud Khalil Museum in Cairo.

The ground also figured in the painting reproduced on the front cover when it was the scene of a fête to celebrate Queen Victoria's Diamond Jubilee.

Camille Pissarro painting the Jubilee fête on Stamford Brook cricket ground from his viewpoint on 'the leads' balcony at the rear of 62 Bath Road.
A possibly unique nineteenth-century photograph of an Impressionist painter at work in the open air. Camille Pissarro painted both an oil (front cover illustration) and a watercolour of the scene. Note the flat iron suspended from the easel to weight it against the wind.

Nearly £1 million was paid for this painting when it was sold at Sotheby's, New York in November 1990

View across Stamford Brook Common **Camille Pissarro, 1897 oil** (private collection)
St. Mary's Church and Stamford Gardens flats can be seen beyond the Common, the allotments in the foreground are alongside the railway. The woman hanging out her washing is probably the level-crossing keeper's wife

Stamford Brook Common, Spring 1996

Bedford Park, Bath Road, La Passarelle, Londres
Camille Pissarro, 1897 oil (private collection)
The footbridge over the Bath Road level crossing, with Stamford Brook Fields beyond, stretching to Starch Green - a view soon to be obscured by housing. Brickmaking had ceased in 1890 and the fields have been cleaned up. The brickwork framing the picture left is probably the newly completed 43 Bath Road

Right:
Bath Road, Londres
Camille Pissarro, 1897 oil
(Ashmolean Museum, Oxford)
Camille Pissarro's granddaughter, Orovida, with her mother, Esther, in the front garden of 62 Bath Road. Seen beyond is 37 Bath Road, then the last occupied house on the north side of the road, and now on the corner of Abinger Road

Below: ***The Train, Bedford Park*** **Camille Pissarro, 1897 oil** (private collection)
'Puffing Jinney' steam train approaching the Bath Road signals, looking south towards Hammersmith & Chiswick Station in Chiswick High Road. St. Peter's church tower can be seen in the background to the left of the telegraph pole (see p.48)

Above*:* ***Stamford Brook Road*** **Ludovic-Rodo Pissarro, 1921** (private collection)
watercolour sketch for etching (see p.5)

Left*:*
The Brook, grey weather
Lucien Pissarro, 1912 oil
(private collection)
Painted from the window of his daughter Orovida's flat at 2 Stamford Gardens (now 26 Stamford Brook Avenue). The maidservant in the garden is probably Emma Ruddock, who worked for the Pissarros for some years, becoming very much one of the family. She continued to correspond with Esther after she married and emigrated to Canada

LUCIEN PISSARRO 1863-1944

Artist, printer and wood engraver, eldest son of Camille Pissarro.

He was born in Paris, and after two earlier visits to England, settled here in 1890, marrying Esther Bensusan in 1892. Living first at Epping, they moved to 62 Bath Road, on the border of Bedford Park, in 1897 when their daughter, and only child, Orovida was three years old. The move to The Brook came in 1902.

Lucien was taught painting by his father and other Impressionist painters, and he was later influenced by the English Fitzroy Street Group, where he was friends with artists such as Spencer Gore and Augustus John, and was a founder member of the Camden Town Group in 1911. He is, however, best known for the beautiful design and the subtle colourings of his wood engravings, many made for the tiny hand-printed books of his Eragny Press.

The Brook type designed by Lucien and used by him from 1903, was named after the house. When the Eragny Press finished he concentrated on painting, working in oils and watercolour, in England and France. At Stamford Brook he painted the Common under snow on several occasions (see pp.10 & 13), and there are paintings of The Brook garden and house. He also painted in Chiswick, Richmond and Acton, where the railway was a favourite subject.

Lucien Pissarro printing on the large hand press at The Brook

ERAGNY PRESS (1894-1914)

The Eragny Press was founded by Lucien Pissarro at a time when the beautiful hand printed English private presses, such as William Morris' Kelmscott Press at Hammersmith, were making a great impact in Britain and on the continent. Lucien used Japanese handmade paper, and the handwritten text was decorated with woodcuts, some in colour. It took long hours of meticulous work, much taken over by Esther as Lucien recovered from his stroke. The war killed the Press. It was impossible to get the right paper, they lost their continental subscribers and costs soared. Thirty-two exquisite books had been printed. There are none on public display at present, but complete sets are in collections at The Ashmolean Museum, Oxford, the British Museum and the Victoria & Albert Museum, London.

Eragny Press frontispiece
E.ET.L.: Esther and Lucien

THE ERAGNY PRESS, «THE BROOK»,
HAMMERSMITH, LONDON, W.
M.D.CCCC.IX.

Top: ***The Brook* type.** Designed by Lucien Pissarro and from 1903 used in the Eragny Press
Bottom: **Motif from *Histoire de la Reine du Matin et de Soliman Prince des Genies***
Eragny Press, 1909

THE PISSARROS AT 'THE BROOK'

Soon after their move from 62 Bath Road to The Brook, Lucien wrote to his father on 30 March 1902: *'Comme tu le vois nous sommes enfin emménagé dans notre Paradis! Nous sommes enchantés de la maison et faisons toute sortes de projets pour l'organisation de notre travail...'* Esther had supervised the months of work. It was the start of a lifetime's obsession for improvements – and of spending money on the house and garden whether or not they could afford it. A major alteration in 1935 (architect: John MacGregor) converted the studio into a separate flat, and entailed demolishing an outside wall which proved particularly costly as it was over the old Stamford brook drain – and the main Stamford brook stream – found eight feet below the floor level, so piers had to be driven, and the bathroom constructed on cantilevers.

The Pissarros were very hospitable, and gave fortnightly Sunday evening soirées for friends, mainly from the art world. By 1910 British avant-garde painters including Gore, Sickert, and Gilman were visiting on Sundays. Orovida had a Siamese cat which used to perch on Lucien's shoulder, whilst he preached the Pissarro doctrine of 'direct painting of the landscape'.

The sitting room at The Brook:
standing, Orovida Pissarro, Lucien Pissarro; seated, Mrs F.L.Bensusan (Esther's mother), Esther Pissarro, Madame Julie Pissarro (Lucien's mother)

Their friend, Dr. van Royan, a Dutch amateur printer of fine books, who died in a concentration camp in 1942, wrote of a Sunday lunch at The Brook in 1914:

> It was like this at the Pissarros, the nice little house is well back from the street ... you go through a white gate and find all sorts of strange and attractive leaves and flowers just like those that appear in his books; on your left is an extension, formerly a stable ... low, small, with four deep windows in which there are all kinds of flowers. On the walls paintings by Camille Pissarro, Lucien Pissarro and others. The dining-room is even smaller. When you sit down there is no room left. On the walls old Japanese woodcuts, engravings by Durer, Ricketts and Pissarro. Above the fireplace are shelves of well-read books – apparently quite extraordinary books to judge by the titles ... Madam is very sweet, yet, very cultured. The daughter is a strange little creature, twenty years old I believe, but looking more like fourteen, plump, very black eyebrows, large, childish eyes and wearing steel spectacles. But she draws extremely well and makes lovely wood-cuts ... We spent the whole day with them and in the evening the room was hardly large enough for all the guests. Pissarro, hidden behind his beard and thick eyebrows, sat there enjoying everything so heartily and yet so quietly. He is an extremely sympathetic man. Refined and very clever, everything he says is well considered and exact, yet at the same time so simple and modest.

Orovida was to become an accomplished artist. But she found no inspiration for her paintings and drawings at Stamford Brook. In March 1922, when she was living in the top floor flat at 2 Stamford Gardens (now 26 Stamford Brook Avenue) looking out over the tennis courts on Stamford Brook Common, she wrote '...I have nearly finished a little painting of tennis players. My models are playing under my window at this moment. They are wonderfully graceful and quite a joy to watch.' But in June she commented '... My tennis players have turned out to be too realistic. I suppose I am too close up to them....' She was 'off for a browse at the British Museum', for it was here and at the London Zoo that she found inspiration for her exotic, Oriental-style, wild and domestic cats.

Lucien was shy and retiring, softly spoken with a gravelly voice and a slight impediment after his stroke. He had rather a derisive sense of humour. Rhoda Bickerdike, Chiswick artist, spoke of the plays the Macgregors staged in the studio at the bottom of Stamford Brook House garden, and remembered a pantomime in which Orovida played a princess – Lucien, with his big black beard, clapping his hands and calling out 'fairies! fairies!' He is remembered in his later years as 'a small man with a long black cloak and terrific white beard, like a very small Father Christmas'. His nephew, David Bensusan-Butt, recalled him smoking Abdullah Salisbury cigarettes in a long holder – the ash would get longer and longer, and then disappear, lost in his great beard.

Right:
Portrait of Lucien Pissarro
J.B. Manson, 1940
(Manchester City Art Galleries)

Below :
The Brook: My Studio Strip
Lucien Pissarro, June 1938
(Ashmolean Museum, Oxford)
The well-stocked garden behind The Brook, with leaning pear tree, still there in 1997 (now propped up)

Esther has been called impossible and lovable. She was stubborn, outspoken, absent-minded, generous in her friendships, a tireless worker, domineering but devoted to Lucien. Both were quite unpractical, and they were continually in financial straits. From time to time they let part of the house to recoup finances.

Sir Alec Guinness occupied the old part of The Brook for six winter months in 1945-6 and remembered it as being 'damned cold'. When the theatre director Tyrone Guthrie came to visit him he said, 'Why didn't you tell me you were living in the prettiest house in London?'

In 1926 Esther learnt to drive, and 'Lizzie', an ancient Ford, was the first of a succession of second-hand cars all called Lizzie or 'the Old Lady'. Her driving could be called eccentric – and she had several accidents, including a collision with a bus at Holland Park. She was summonsed for dangerous driving, but found not guilty, and the bus company paid for the car repair.

The Brook cottage beyond Stamford Brook Open Space, with its clipped hedges and well-kept appearance c.1935. The north-east corner of the Hammersmith/Chiswick boundary curled around The Brook cottage, where there are three old boundary stones. The boundary was straightened being redrawn along Stamford Brook Road in the 1994 changes, since when the 'Open Space' (which was in Hammersmith), has become part of Chiswick (Borough of Hounslow). Its neat appearance disappeared long ago

CHISWICK HIGH ROAD

The Coach and Horses

Demolished 1900

Good-bye to an Old Wayside Inn

The Coach and Horses, an old wayside inn facing the Chiswick-road, near Turnham-green, is now being demolished, and with it and the laying out of the adjoining market gardens for building upon, goes the last vestige of the rural road from London to Gunnersbury. Until quite recent years hedgerows and barns occupied the sites of the adjacent shops by the junction of the Goldhawk-road with the Chiswick-road at the spot called 'Young's Corner', but the district has now been altered so greatly that it is nothing more than an extension of London. Old times and now are in sharp contrast in the pulling down of the humble old roadside inn and the building of a palatial new one behind it, operations going forward simultaneously. It was never a house named in story or legend, but with the drivers of the market carts and the hay waggons pulling up at the roadside water-trough, beneath the swinging sign, to give their horses a drink, it greatly resembled one of Morland's characteristic old pictures of rural life.

Daily News 16 August 1900

Purchased by Messrs Watney & Co. and completely rebuilt, it remained The Coach and Horses for many years. After several recent modernisations it is now Nachos Mexican Bar and Restaurante.

YOUNG'S CORNER

'Young's Corner' – at the junction of King Street and Goldhawk Road – has been a fare stage since the days of horse-drawn trams. It was named after Charles Spencer Young, a grocer and antiquarian – one of several generations of Youngs – who ran the corner shop in the nineteenth century.

Writing in 1926, Walter Corwen of Dukes Avenue, Chiswick, remembered it was 'improved with more modern shop windows by the late Mr.Young. It was a decent grocer's shop and also a Post Office. I well remember the business, for as a boy of about fifteen years (1870) I opened an account in the Post Office Savings Bank...'

Charles Young had acquired a good collection of prints, and when he retired he displayed them in his shop windows for the enjoyment of passers by, including an anonymous correspondent to *The Times* in 1958, who had boyhood memories of Young's Corner in 1890 – seventy years earlier!: 'In the window the things that attracted my boy's attention most were eighteenth-century coloured caricatures by Gillray and Rowlandson, and so on, framed in black.'

Young's Corner 1880
Young's grocers and post office on the right, the farmstead known as Bagley's Cottage or The Gardens on the left, with thirteen acres of market garden stretching beyond to the north

Young's Corner was rebuilt in 1894, when the whole area was developed. Already known as 'Young's Corner', Mr.Young's name is immortalised in a plaque beneath the decorative Victorian pinnacle.

The shop soon became a 'gentleman's outfitters', first run by a Mr. Ensoll, and after he retired in 1926, by Reginald Hill, who remained in business for nearly sixty years. It is now a Fullers' 'off licence'.

1890-1902
DEVELOPMENT OF GOLDHAWK ROAD/ CHISWICK HIGH ROAD/ PREBEND GARDENS

The farmhouse on the north-west side was at the time of development occupied by Arthur Robbins with thirteen acres of orchard and market garden stretching north. Over five acres, up to the railway (now the District Line) viaduct, were acquired in 1890 by John Carter of Dalling Road, to build shops and private houses, and he was also to make the road called Prebend Gardens.

The first houses along the west side of the Goldhawk Road were completed in 1891. The year is inscribed along house nos. 368 to 400, with decorative terracotta brickwork. On the rooftop of nos. 388 and 392 are two handsome eagles – goldhawks perhaps? The Chiswick High Road shops were fronted by a wide pavement (they still are), and this stretch of road was named The Pavement.

The Church Commissioners' rules and regulations to tenants were strict, particularly for prospective traders. Mr. Carter was instructed that there should be 'no noxious, noisome, or offensive trade or business, nor the sale of wine, beer or spirits...' In May 1897 application for an 'off licence' for a beers, wine and spirits merchant, was made by Messrs. Haig for a shop under construction, but the Church Commissioners were 'not prepared to waive the restriction against such use of premises'. In March 1900 a similar application made by Messrs Edell & Gordon of 32 The Pavement was also refused. However, the application two years later by John Timmis, a chemist, and tenant of J.B Sainsbury, of no. 10 The Pavement, to sell medicated wines met with cautious permission, provided his sales were strictly confined to medicated wines, which 'may include such articles as Halls Cocoa Wine or Wincarnis'. Timmis became Timmis & Gould (*Mr. Gould was known as 'Goofy Gould'. Why, I don't know!)* – now the Pestle & Mortar.

The COMMODORE

Opened 1929

The Proscenium

The Italian Alcoves

The Vestibule

The Console

London's Supreme Talkie Theatre

The Commodore, opposite Young's Corner, was one of the finest cinemas in London and claimed to be the first in England designed specially for 'talkies'. The foundation stone was laid by the well-known American film star, Tallulah Bankhead on 1 January 1929, and my wife attended the grand opening night in September the same year.

In the 1930s there were always queues waiting for every show, which included two films, a stage show, the news, and of course the large organ which rose out of the orchestra pit with the famous Harry Davidson at the keyboard. Prices ranged from 3/6 down to 9d at matinees. The children's Saturday morning programme cost 6d and was always packed.

There was a pleasant tea and coffee lounge on the first floor with waitress service.

MECCA BINGO HALL 1965-1979

Demolished 1982

RAILWAYS

NORTH AND SOUTH WESTERN JUNCTION RAILWAY, BRANCH LINE

Since it was only in 1966 that the track was taken up and the gates of the level crossing were removed, many residents still remember the railway line which led from the old coal yard at Chiswick High Road, parallel with Prebend Gardens through what is now Ravensmede and Welstead Way, over a level crossing in Bath Road, and northwards between Abinger and Emlyn Roads to South Acton.

The second half of the nineteenth century witnessed a frenzied building of railways all over the country, and this was the first in our area – a branch line of the North and South Western Junction Railway. It started in 1857 as a goods service, and the following year became a passenger service, connecting with the NSWJ's line at Acton Gatehouse Junction (just north of the railway bridge, then a level crossing, in Acton Lane). Originally a single carriage was detached from the rear of the North London trains from Camden Town to Old Kew – sometimes performed without stopping the train, the guard snatching the coupling as the train slowed down – but by the end of October 1865 this was replaced by a separate train.

The station in Chiswick High Road, at the entrance to what is now Ravensmede, consisted of a private house. It was originally called Hammersmith Station, although it was plainly in Chiswick; and it was renamed Hammersmith and Chiswick in July 1880. The *West London Observer*, which published the local railway timetables, always referred to it as 'the North London Station at Turnham Green'.

There were trains to 'Acton, Kilburn, Hampstead Road, Camden Road, Islington, Kingsland, Hackney, Bow, Stepney, Fenchurch Street, and all stations on the Blackwall Railway'. For a few years this rather circuitous route provided businessmen from Hammersmith and Chiswick with transport to the City, replacing the rather slow and uncomfortable horse buses. The so-called 'express' trains took some fifty-five minutes. There were nine trains a day, with a reduced service on Sundays. The branch line had been constructed by the company outside the guaranteed capital, without the authorization of the shareholders, who reported after an enquiry that the capital account had been 'grossly misused', and they could find no reason for the construction of the branch since there were no likely sources of traffic in that area. They were proved right. It was economically viable for only a few years, as alternative routes to the City opened from Hammersmith and Shepherd's Bush (the twopenny tube). Only crowded on Boat Race days, it managed however to survive providing a passenger service until January 1917.

The 'Puffing Jinney' or 'Little Jinney' steam train, as portrayed in Camille Pissarro's painting (see p.35), ran up and down the line for over fifty years from 1857-1909. A few years before the First World War an attempt was made to encourage local passengers by making three Halts between the High Road and South Acton, one at Bath Road and the others at Woodstock Road and Rugby Road.

My wife used to travel from the Halt in Woodstock Road near her home to the High Road. As a child, her fare was a halfpenny, and she would also travel the other way via South Acton round to Kew Gardens.

The train consisted of an engine and two coaches, with a driver and guard. It was all very friendly, as the guard would hold the train if he saw the children with a parent making for the steps to the Halt.

A coal depot had been created alongside the station, and when the passenger service ceased the line was maintained for coal traffic and deliveries to builders' merchants. The level crossing was still in use, and vehicles along the Bath Road would be stopped for several minutes when the crossing gates were closed. There was a small brick built building on the south-east side in which the crossing keeper lived, known appropriately as Railway Cottage.

INCIDENT ON THE RAILWAY LINE DEATH OF RUSSIAN REVOLUTIONARY

In December 1895 exiled Russian revolutionary Sergius Michaelovitch Kravchinsky known as Stepniak, who was living in Bedford Park, crossed the stile leading to the open level crossing at Woodstock Road, deep in thought and oblivious of the engine-driver's warning whistle. He was struck by a train and killed. The Coroner's court passed a verdict of 'Accidental Death' and called for a bridge to be built over the crossing, and until then a man should be stationed to warn pedestrians of approaching trains. Stepniak's funeral at Woking Crematoriam was attended by thousands.

The footbridge was duly built.

Bath Road level crossing, 1933 looking south
Railway Cottage on the left, signal box and 62 Bath Road on the right. The two posts are all that remain of the footbridge, which was in use until about 1930

1965 CLOSURE OF THE NSWJ RAILWAY

With the decrease in the use of coal for heating, the Hammersmith and Chiswick goods depot finally closed in May 1965 (part of the Beeching Plan), ending 'Soapsud Alley', as the line had been nicknamed by the laundry workers who had once travelled to work at South Acton – 'Soapsuds Island'.

In 1966 the track was taken up and the level crossing gates removed. North of the level crossing flats were built by an enterprising group of families, doing most of the work themselves at the weekends. Ravensmede Estate was built on land south of the District Line viaduct in 1977. Ambitious – and less acceptable – schemes for the area north from the viaduct to the Bath Road were rejected.

In 1962 a proposal by the Railway Sites Company to build a piazza development including a 10-storey block of flats, 8-storey office block, bowling alley, supermarket and twenty-three shops was turned down following a 400-signature protest petition and a public enquiry. After lengthy negotiations Hounslow bought the land from British Rail in 1969, but their plan to build an extension to Chiswick Polytechnic was by then not viable, and there had been more protests as houses were to be demolished for exits. It became a municipal car park in 1973, heavily used by commuters, but nevertheless the land was sold to the Notting Hill Housing Trust, and thirty-one homes were completed in 1996. The new street named Welstead Way commemorates the nineteenth-century Lords of the Prebendal Manor.

August 1965
Above:
Bath Road level crossing with derelict signal box
Right:
Looking south along the over-grown tracks (now Ravensmede) to Prebend Mansions in Chiswick High Road

The former N&SWJ station in Chiswick High Road. Originally converted from a private house it reverted again to private use when passenger services ceased in 1917. In the 1970s it was a tv repair shop. This house and the coal merchants alongside the old entrance to the goods yard were all demolished when Ravensmede was built

THE DISTRICT LINE

The other railway in the area is, of course, still functioning, and is commonly called the District Line. It started life as part of the London and South Western Railway in 1869, and was originally known as the Kensington and Richmond Railway. Shaftesbury Road station was opened in 1873 (renamed Ravenscourt Park in 1888), but there was no station at Stamford Brook until 1912.

When I first travelled to the City, there was only one 'island' platform, that now used for westbound traffic. The eastbound platform was constructed on the Vaughan Avenue side in 1932 to provide for the extension of the Piccadilly Line, which runs on the two central tracks, so that our original eastbound platform is but rarely used on the odd occasion that westbound Piccadilly trains make a stop.

In those days there was a choice of 1st and 2nd class carriages – and only a few of them were non-smoking.

TRAVELLING ON THE DISTRICT LINE FROM CHARING CROSS (EMBANKMENT) TO STAMFORD BROOK IN 1920

from *The House by the River*, a novel by A.P.Herbert (who lived on Hammersmith Mall, thinly disguised as Hammerton Chase, the home of civil servant, John Egerton)

Every misfortune which can happen to a man who travels Underground in London had happened to John Egerton. Worn and irritable with a sultry day at the Ministry he had jostled with a shuffling multitude on to the airless platform at Charing Cross. From near the bottom of the stairs he saw that an Ealing train was already in; more important, the train was stopping at Stamford Brook. Stamford Brook was a 'non-stop station', so that if you missed your train in the busy hours you might wait for an intolerable time. Already they were slamming home the doors, he had only to swing himself in. Then from nowhere appeared a youthful uniformed official, who barred the way with an infuriating aspect of authority, and slammed fast the receding door. The train slid clattering past and vanished with a parting flicker of blue flashes.

The next train was a Wimbledon one; the next an Inner Circle; the next a Richmond, not stopping at Stamford Brook. The endless people shuffled down the stairs, drifted aimlessly along the platform, jostled and barged good-humouredly about the teeming trains. Government flappers giggled in small groups, furtively examined by ambulant young men. Why was Stamford Brook a non-stop station? Hundreds of people used it - far more than Sloane Square, for example, or St.James's Park. He would write a letter to the Company about these things.

The Ealing train came in, and John was swept in with a tight mass of people through the middle doors of a smoking carriage. The atmosphere was a suffocating mixture of hot breath and evil tobacco-smoke. The carriage was packed. Men and women stood jammed together like troops in a communication-trench. Here and there a clerk stood up with a sheepish mumble and a sallow woman sank thankfully into his seat. John stared with increasing resentment at the rows of men who did not get up - tired labourers in corduroy trousers who sat on in unmoved contentment, or gross men with cigars who screened themselves behind evening papers, pretending they did not notice the standing women...

At Earl's Court the crowd melted a little; there were no seats, but there was room to breathe - room to stand by oneself, free from the pressure of strange bodies. At Baron's Court he crept into a seat. At Hammersmith a noisy mob of shopgirls and hobbledehoys surged in, and he surrendered his seat to a young woman, who was munching something. She sat down with a giggle and took her sister on her lap. Only two more stations.

The lights were out now. The train ran out through the daylight on to a high embankment, past an interminable series of dingy houses. There was more air. The filthy smoke eddied out of the narrow windows. The train rocked enormously - a bad piece of line. Looking down the car from his place by the door, John saw through the haze an interminable vista of uniform right hands fiercely clinging to uniform straps, of right arms uniformly crooked, of bowed heads uniformly bent over evening papers, of endless backs uniformly enduring and dull. And as the train gave a great lurch, all the elbows swung out together towards the windows, and all the bodies bent outward like willows in the wind, and all the heads were lifted together in a mute and uniform protest. It was all like some fantastic physical drill. Then he fell into the weary stupor of the habitual Underground traveller, listening semi-consciously to the insane chatter of the chuckling girls. Ravenscourt Park shot by unnoticed.

Stooping suddenly he saw the familiar letters of Stamford Brook dashing past at an astonishing speed. Surely - surely the train was stopping. The porters' room - the ticket collector - the passenger-shelter - the Safety First pictures - the advertisement of What Ho! the other name-board of the station - the whole station - shot maddeningly past. The train rushed on to the intolerable remoteness of Turnham Green. Hell! From Turnham Green you might walk home; but it took nearly twenty minutes. Or if you were lucky you caught a train quickly back to Stamford Brook.

Plus ça change!

BUSES

In 1855 the London General Omnibus Company (LGOC) was formed to amalgamate the many small bus companies which had proliferated since the introduction of the London omnibus in 1829, and by the following year they had taken over 600 of the 810 London companies.

The LGOC had stabling for some of their horses in Stamford Brook Road opposite The Queen of England pub from 1877 until 1909, by which time the horse was being replaced by the petrol engine.

Now Owen Conway, a Renault repair garage, the premises still display the LGOC initials in raised stonework to the left of the entrance arch.

The journey by horse bus along the Bath Road and Stamford Brook Road – the route followed today by the diesel engined bus – is remembered by Sybil Pearce in her *Edwardian Childhood in Bedford Park.* Aged 96 in 1996, Sybil Pearce still lives in Bedford Park.

> Some of my favourite days were those on which my Mother decided to go 'up to town' shopping. We would catch a two-horse drawn omnibus in the Bath Road outside the Tabard Inn and my great joy was to seat myself just behind the driver on the top of the 'bus in the front seat. I remember one driver in particular - a fat, red haired man wearing green woollen mittens. I loved the way he brandished his whip and clucked his teeth at the horses. It took us an hour to get to Queen's Road, Bayswater - where we shopped at Whiteleys - because we changed horses on the way but, unfortunately, I cannot remember at which particular place. If it rained we were covered with black mackintosh covers lined with tartan, which, when placed over me, came up under my chin; so I never remember getting wet.

Ludovic-Rodo Pissarro, Lucien Pissarro's younger brother, who lived for some years in England, and who bought 3 Blenheim Road, Bedford Park, living there at times during 1921-5, made an etching of the open-topped motor bus to Acton Green in 1921, as it passed Stamford Brook Common (see pp.5 & 36).

The local bus running the lengthy route from Acton Green, via Shepherd's Bush, Oxford Circus, Trafalgar Square to Mitcham, cost 8d and took 102 minutes. It was for many years an 88 – notorious for its infrequent service – although it was meant to run every 8 minutes. In 1990 London Transport halved the route and renumbered it 94 at our end. The service, still infrequent, is run by London United.

TRAMS

Early trams were horse drawn, the rails giving a smooth journey and they were able to haul a heavier load than the horse buses. Tracks were laid along the Goldhawk Road and the High Road by the West Metropolitan Tramways Co. in 1882 to open their routes from Shepherd's Bush to Young's Corner and from Young's Corner west along the High Road to Kew Bridge.

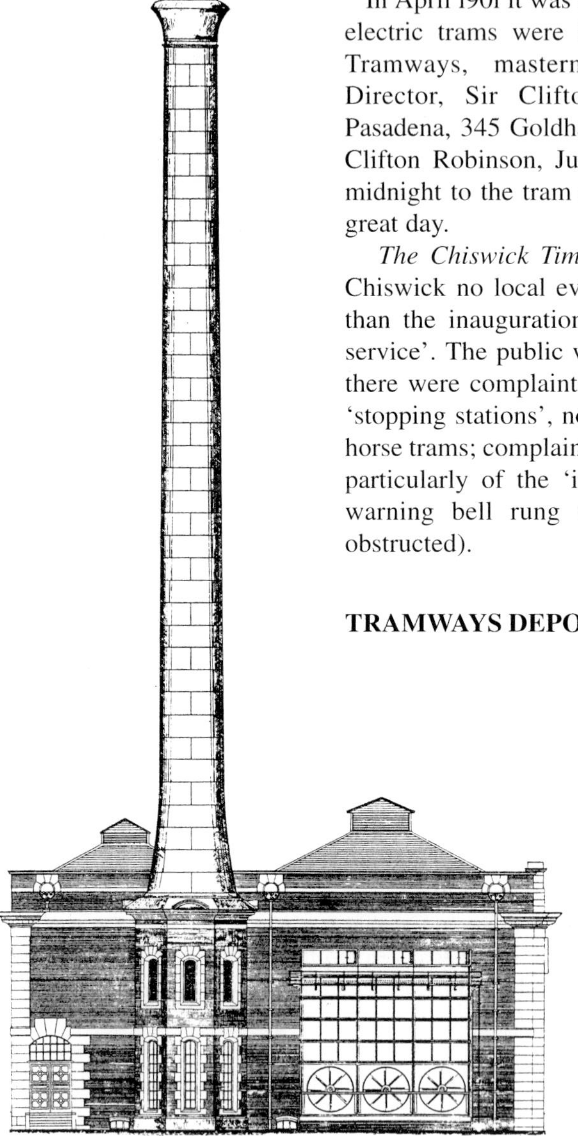

In April 1901 it was on this route that London's first electric trams were introduced by London United Tramways, masterminded by their Managing Director, Sir Clifton Robinson, who lived at Pasadena, 345 Goldhawk Road, and whose son, Mr. Clifton Robinson, Junior, had given tuition around midnight to the tram drivers to prepare them for the great day.

The Chiswick Times declared: 'In the history of Chiswick no local event has caused more sensation than the inauguration of the new electric tramway service'. The public were generally enthusiastic, but there were complaints that the new trams only used 'stopping stations', not pulling up anywhere like the horse trams; complaints too of the noise and dust, and particularly of the 'incessant tin-kettle gongs' (the warning bell rung when the car's passage was obstructed).

TRAMWAYS DEPOT, CHISWICK HIGH ROAD

From 1887 West Metropolitan Tramways had its main depot north of Chiswick High Road, which became the headquarters of London United Tramways in 1901 with a large Power House (a listed building, now converted into flats).

This lofty, single-storey edifice was divided into gleaming engine and boiler rooms with a 260 foot high steel smoke-stack, demolished in 1966. The depot is now Stamford Brook Bus Garage.

Young's Corner, c.1905. At the junction where electric trams from Shepherd's Bush met those from Hammersmith, the Shepherd's Bush to Kew Bridge tram is turning right into Chiswick High Road, whilst the tram to Hounslow from Hammersmith waits in the main road. Kerkham, the drapers, is on the left, opposite Ensolls, gentlemen's outfitters

The last tram drove down Chiswick High Road on 26 October 1935. Trams were replaced by trolleybuses.

The trolleybus terminus at Stamford Brook Station, Goldhawk Road, 14 April 1962, a few weeks before trolleybuses were superceded by the diesel engined bus. The conductor is transferring the two trolley poles from the through-running wires to those of the turning circle.

GOLDHAWK ROAD
OAKBROOK and the BRANDONS

A stylish Gothic villa built in 1831 by George Scott of Ravenscourt to front the 'intended new branch mail road', and the south wing of the house remains today in its original form. In 1861 Oakbrook became the home of the newly married Gabriel Samuel Brandon and his young Bavarian wife Cecile Lion. Brandon was a successful London solicitor, whose clients included the French actress, Sarah Bernhardt who stayed with them on her visits to London. The Brandons lavishly furnished the house with antique furniture, bronzes and objets d'art, some being ordered from Paris. It was probably in 1872-3 that they extended the front of the main wing and added a large top storey and a tower to this already large mansion. Cecile had thirteen children (not all survived), and their daughter Lilian was to marry William Bull (see p.26). Gabriel died in 1888 leaving Cecile with a large, young family. She lived another forty years, working indefatigably for good causes, and was founder and president of many local institutions.

Right:
The morning room at Oakbrook, 1908

When Cecile died in 1926, the furniture and effects were sold at a huge three-day auction, the antiques realising large sums. The house was bought by Queen Charlotte's Hospital and became their administrative section.

INVERMEAD, the villa to the south, was demolished to build the new hospital, and maternity wards were built over the old Stamford brook where it crossed towards Ravenscourt between Oakbrook and Invermead.

QUEEN CHARLOTTE'S MATERNITY HOSPITAL

Founded in 1752 in Jermyn Street and moving in 1813 to Marylebone Road, it was one of the earliest lying-in hospitals in England. In 1929 a special unit was set up in Hammersmith for treatment of puerperal 'childbed' fever. Building was still in progress, but the whole hospital was hastily moved to its new site in September 1940 as the bombing of London began. The research department has now moved to Hammersmith Hospital, and the maternity hospital itself may follow. Oakbrook, a grade II listed building, will survive – the future for the other buildings is uncertain.

Nearby the **ROYAL MASONIC HOSPITAL**, an architectural prizewinner when it was opened in 1933, has been closed. It may become luxury apartments – but its future too is undecided. Next to Queen Charlotte's, the large block of flats, **STAMFORD COURT**, was also built in the 1930s, after the villas up to Ravenscourt Gardens were demolished.

Oakbrook, Goldhawk Road 1997

Gothic carriage house with battlements at 2 Rylett Road, built c.1890. Photographed in 1983, before its conversion into an attractive residence, retaining the Gothic facade. Architect Peter Faggetter. Immediately opposite, behind 1 Rylett Road, is another derelict, castellated folly, built as stables at about the same time

TWENTIETH-CENTURY DEVELOPMENT SOUTH OF THE COMMON

In May 1898 architect and surveyor J.A. Gill Knight, obtained a 999 year lease from the Church Commissioners of about 12½ acres south of Stamford Brook Common (Stamford Brook Estate) to build blocks of residential flats or semi-detached houses.

Stamford Brook Mansions, Goldhawk Rd. (mansion flats)	built 1901
Linkenholt Mansions, Stamford Brook Avenue	1902-3
Hauteville Court Gardens, Stamford Brook Common	1903
Ranelagh Gardens, Stamford Brook Avenue	1903-4
Vaughan Avenue (houses) even nos. 2-16, odd nos. 1-7	1904-7
Pleydell Avenue (houses: builders L.J. & J.W. Martin)	1905-10

By October 1905 14 blocks of flats and 16 houses had been built, many remaining unlet. Here as elsewhere the call for flats was not as high as expected, even with the advent of the electric tram. An important factor was that the District Line station did not open until 1912. The Church Commissioners commented: 'The houses he has built would we think most likely have been sold or let sometime ago if the roads had been completed so as to provide satisfactory means of access to them. Under his agreement all the roads should have been completed by Christmas 1901.' The building of further mansion flats, planned to extend along the south of the Common, was abandoned. By 1906 Gill Knight was heavily mortgaged to financier Selwood Cooke Riddle (died 1911), and practically bankrupt by 1911. In 1911 the builder Leonard J. Martin was also in serious financial difficulties. Building continued for Riddle Estates Ltd:

Prebend Gardens
(south of viaduct, part of Young's Corner development 1893-4)
north of railway viaduct (known as Ilton Road 1908-10):

odd nos. 83-97	built 1908
even nos. (E.side) 60-74, 42-48	1910-14
" 50-60	1921-2
99	1927
South Side 6-13 (developer: F.L.Britton)	1925-6

In 1923 Henry John Coleman, the father of author Reginald Coleman, took over the building lease for what became:

South Side 2-5	built 1926-7
Prebend Gardens odd nos. 47-83	1924-9
Stamford Brook Ave: odd nos. 1-7,17,19, even nos. 2-10	1926
(tennis club site) odd nos. 9-15 (developer: P.G.Parkman)	1933-4

The houses in Stamford Brook Avenue were originally all named. Numbers were introduced in the 1950s. East side: Louise Villa, Hilltress, Turbery, Merriville, Leafwood; West side: Maxwelton, Woodgarth, Looe, Twysdene, Brookside, Glenrive, Jesslyn, Lyndhurst, Casita, Kandersteg. I was amused by the choice of Maxwelton (it became no. 1) which was bought by a Mr. & Mrs. Laurie, and she was Annie. The famous song Annie Laurie *says* ''Maxwelton braes are bonny'.

REGINALD COLEMAN
ON THE CHANGES OVER THE LAST SEVENTY YEARS

CARS

The most obvious change, which is a national difference, is the ownership of private cars – and the resultant problem of parking, especially where there are large blocks of flats which when built did not provide garaging or parking facilities. In 1926 there were no more than twenty cars owned around Stamford Brook Avenue , belonging to the occupiers of houses with garages or using the six lock-ups which my father had built (now the northern end of the petrol station). One or two cars belonged to flat tenants, but it was unusual to see more than a few parked in the road.

HOUSE AND FLAT OWNERSHIP

With regard to flats – in those days all occupiers were tenants – the buying of a flat did not happen until after the war. The population was not so transient as today, and one got to know one's neighbours quite well, since many of the occupiers of both houses and flats were there for twenty years or more. Prices for rent or purchase varied but little - and being on Church Commissioners' land, was leasehold only.

Flats & Apartments Unfirnished Stamford Brook Avenue - Unfurnished suites of 3 rooms from 7s to 10s 6d p.w. Two minutes from trams (Rylett Rd) facing Common - Apply Caretaker, No.2* Stamford Brook Avenue, Goldhawk Road
West London Observer 10 June 1912

*now no.22 Stamford Brook Avenue

STAMFORD BROOK - Semi-detached modern residence, six bedrooms, two reception, kitchen; lease 73 yrs; good garden; vacant possession; £1,350 - Morton and Waters, 310 King Street, Hammersmith
West London Observer 5 April 1929

ST. MARY'S COURT, W.6.
One, two and three-bedroom flats, prices £82,500 to £147,500 Hallet & Lines & Co. Estate Agents & Surveyors 1987

PLEYDELL AVENUE, W.6
Six/seven bedroom family house, 2 reception, fitted kitchen, 2 bathrooms, west-facing garden, Freehold £375,000 Foxtons February 1997

St. Mary's Court 1986. The exterior of the church has been retained, the interior is now five floors of one, two and three-bedroom flats

SHOPS

The womenfolk would know most of the shopkeepers by name – menfolk less so, since we all worked a five and a half day week, and of course hardly any shop opened on a Sunday.

There were no supermarkets or chain stores and everybody tended to shop mainly within walking distance, so we enjoyed what can be described as a village atmosphere. On entering a shop my wife would be greeted with a 'Good morning Mrs. C' and she would reply 'Good morning Mr. X'. At the end of the purchase, there would often be added the question, Would you like me to deliver, Mrs.C?

There was a group of small shops on the Goldhawk Road, opposite the Queen of England, covering a wide variety of trades, and there were more shops from Ravenscourt Gardens up to Young's Corner.

Mr. Higgins and Mr. Rogers (later Mr. Deninson), in their tiny shops next to The Raven, were the last of the Goldhawk Road shops to disappear in the late 1970s.

1952 Street Directory

GOLDHAWK ROAD-
=*Ravenscourt Sq.*
319 Knight Hector boot repr
321 Bleckwen Edwd tobcnst
323&325 Hapgood Mrs CMCafe
327a Miller LW watch repr

=*Ravenscourt Gardens*
371 Higgins Leonard Alfd. grocer
373 Rogers Henry John, boot repr
375 *The Raven* P.H. Stanley B Pleydell
=*Here the Railway crosses*

383 Aiton Mrs Eliz florist
383 Heywood A&Son plumber
397 Blackburn Wm blder
401a Oliffe Geo bldr
403 Wright Mrs AE ladies hrdrsr
407 Collins Isaac&Sons,tailor
409 Goula Leslie Chas, chemist
411 Sparks Wm Hr boot repr
413 Burley AG&Co, jewellers
415 RPCleaners, dyers & cleanrs
=*Young's Corner*

Then on the main road, on either side of Young's Corner, there were several butchers, the Home and Colonial for butter, margarine and cheese (perhaps the first of the chain stores), as well as a haberdashery, a dress shop, a chemist and the But and Ben café. There was also a general hardware store which sold paraffin. One must remember that at that time the main heating was coal in open fires, aided by the paraffin stove. There were several coal merchants' offices at the old coal yard on what is now Ravensmede.

Coal brings back memories of the dense London fogs from which we suffered every winter. I remember trying to drive back from a dance at Chiswick Town Hall (my parents were among the small minority of those who owned a car), and the fog was so dense that I had to drive along the High Road with dipped headlamps following the tram lines. Unfortunately, when the track turned sharp to the left, I thought we were at Young's Corner and followed, only to hear a voice from the darkness 'Where the ... do you think you're going?' I had driven into the then tram depot, now Stamford Brook Bus Garage.

PERSONALITIES

Among the tradesmen known to a large number of the community was Harry Laxton, who had the newspaper stand at Stamford Brook Station. He won the M.M. and the Croix de Guerre in the 1914-18 war and lived next to the station. He was a great horse-racing man and many a time I saw a taxi waiting for him with the engine running, waiting to get him to a not-too-distant course such as Sandown Park or Brighton for the first race. He died a few years after the Second World War, and the stand was taken over by his son Albert, who retired after over forty years in 1988.

Another family with long connections were the Nixsons, who owned the newsagent, tobacconist and sweet shop near the Queen of England. The Nixson family over several generations ran the business for some eighty years until 1967. Grandmother Nixson sold her homemade icecream in Victorian glass dishes, and served coffee from a long trestle table to the drivers of horsedrawn vehicle – many no doubt from the LGOC stables opposite. We could buy our newspapers by the 88 bus stop – on the London-bound side of the road.

Goldhawk Road October 1957
Higgins Stores, grocer, and H.J. Rogers, boot repairer, next to *The Raven.*
District Line viaduct on right

LEISURE PASTIMES

I suppose going to the cinema was probably the most popular leisure pastime, and many people went at least once a week. As well as The Commodore at Young's Corner (see p.46) before the war there was also the small Park Cinema opposite Starch Green.

We used to enjoy going to the Lyric Theatre, Hammersmith, where Nigel Playfair's productions were outstanding, and I particularly remember The Beggar's Opera. *We used to sit in the gallery in those days, which at the Lyric was very comfortable. The Chiswick Empire, in Chiswick High Road opposite Turnham Green, was one of the top variety theatres in London. I remember taking my mother to see Max Miller, 'the cheeky chappie', who came on stage with his very loud check suit, fast talk and very blue language – not the best choice for mother!*

We had 'the wireless' and had progressed from the cat's whisker period to sets with valves, but listening in did not have the effect on entertainment that television was to have in the 1950s.

TENNIS

Tennis was very popular. Locally, in addition to the six public grass courts on Stamford Brook Common, there were three tennis clubs: The Stamfordian Club, Stamford Brook Club, and Hartswood Lawn Tennis Club.

The small Stamfordian Club on what is now the Scout Hut land off Stamford Brook Station Approach (renamed Wilson Walk in 1993) had only three courts. Although permission had been granted for play on public courts on Sunday afternoons, it was not permitted by the Church Commissioners, despite continuing pleas by the Club Secretary. Writing in February 1923 he begged them:

> ...to allow us to use our courts say for two hours only from either 2-4pm or 3-5pm... In many cases late working hours prevent them [the members] being able to play for long on midweek evenings, whilst their keenness and zest is not the same as that 'freedom-from-official duties' feeling experienced on the fuller days... if the Commissioners do not make this concession the Club will be forced into liquidation.

Eventually in July 1928 permission was granted for Sunday play – but it was too late to save the club, which closed at the end of that season. It became Scout Haven, HQ for the 3rd Chiswick Group of Boy Scouts in 1929, later with a new HQ replacing the old pavilion.

In Stamford Brook Avenue on land now belonging to nos. 9, 11, 13 and 15 there was the Stamford Brook Club for residents of the Stamford Brook Estate, with a small wooden pavilion and two red hard courts. I was a member from 1926 to 1930, when it closed down and the houses were built.

HARTSWOOD LAWN TENNIS CLUB

North, in Hartswood Road, was the Hartswood Lawn Tennis Club, with six grass courts, which still flourishes today with floodlit hard courts and a new pavilion. I joined, with several others in 1930, on the closure of the Stamford Brook Club, and was Captain in 1938 and 1946-52.

The Club opened in the summer of 1914, and the original pavilion (destroyed by fire December 1985) was a pre-fabricated building first erected for the White City Exhibition in 1908, which was subsequently sold off, transferred and re-erected in 1914 as a pavilion for the newly formed tennis club. The land was owned, leasehold, by the Rassell family who had a florist's shop in Earl's Court and to the north of the tennis club they had their nursery garden and glass houses for flower growing to supply the shop. In 1925 Charles Rassell built a new pavilion, which the following year became his private residence, The Garden House. The area set aside for more courts became his garden. The house was demolished in the 1980s. At Hartswood too Sunday afternoon play was not permitted until 1926, nor winter play on Sunday mornings until 1934 – something we take very much for granted today.

Dan Maskell, then the leading professional at Queen's Club, with his partner, A.J. Pearce, were invited to Hartswood in 1931. William Macmillan ('Mac') and I, as first couple in the men's team, took them on – winning the first set whilst they acclimatised to the notorious bad bounces! After which they were always at the net and we hardly got another game.

Members of the newly formed Hartswood Lawn Tennis Club, Summer 1914
The pavilion is a pre-fabricated building from the White City Exhibition

THE SECOND WORLD WAR

Stamford Brook had very few casualties and suffered little damage in comparison with Chiswick, but the residents were not to know this as the air raid siren sounded almost nightly during the winter months of 1940.

There was an ARP Post in the children's playground at the corner of Prebend Gardens, the tennis courts on Stamford Brook Common became vegetable allotments and at the west end of the Common there were two large underground air raid shelters. Doris Price, who has lived at 12 South Side since 1941, remembers: 'We had forms down each side of the shelter, and an old bucket behind a curtain at the far end. We used to take a blanket over with us and lie down on the forms to sleep. After a while it got very damp, and we used our Morrison shelter in the kitchen.'

There was a mobile gun on the NSWJ Railway. Doris Price: 'It used to go backwards and forwards, and we used to hear the terrific whacks. It gave us a feeling we were hitting back.'

STAMFORD BROOK BOMBED

Information from the ARP Wardens' Incident Book:
25 September 1940 Time: 2150 High Explosive bomb
9 South Side, back. House demolished, minor damage to eight others. No casualties.
64 Prebend Gardens, roadway. Minor damage to sixteen houses in Prebend Gardens and to the gas service pipe. Incendiary bombs fell in Bath Road and Pleydell Avenue. Minor damage only.
Doris Price, who only ten days previously had moved out of 9 South Side where she had been lodging: 'The front of the house was quite OK and the back was sliced off like a piece of rich fruit cake – and it had all crumbled'. The old lady who lived there was away.

3 November 1940 Time: 1710 High Explosive
77-79 Prebend Gardens Casualties: Fatal 0 Hospital 2 Minor 6
Houses demolished, adjoining houses uninhabitable, lesser damage others. Siren not sounded until 1723 hours.
Wanda Sala, who was an air raid warden and living in Linkenholt Mansions: 'It was a Sunday afternoon after a quiet period, and quite foggy, when we heard this "chug, chug, chug" of the plane approaching very low, and we rushed on to the balcony to watch. The place shook as the bomb dropped, and we all dashed on duty, worried about casualties. Only one woman and child were at home, and had dived under the table, which saved them, but I believe the woman died soon after. Water was gushing out in the road, and the brook had to be repiped.' When 75 to 81 Prebend Gardens were rebuilt in 1947 their gable frontages were omitted.

On 12 November 1940 a bomb in Emlyn Road demolished numbers 33 and 35, with 31 badly damaged. All rebuilt after the war. Nearby, Chiswick Polytechnic in Bath Road was partly destroyed by a flying bomb one August morning in 1944. One person was killed and many hurt. Thirty-four families had to be rehoused.

A SENSE OF COMMUNITY?

In concluding, we ask what is it that forges a community spirit?

Nothing brings people together so surely as a war, or a disaster, or a possible threat to an established way of life, and the area has had its share over the years. A letter survives from 1873, signed by the three householders at the north-east of the Common, protesting to the Court Leet of the Manor of Fulham about the nuisance caused by gypsies camping on the Common; a similar situation arose some years ago when gypsies took up residence on the derelict children's playground. From time to time residents have combined to react against noise from the railway: in 1911 caused by shunting in the goods yard at 3am, in 1989 by blaring loudspeaker announcements. Our current threat *is* affecting our use of the car, as commuters daily take all the parking spaces along our streets. Parking of another kind – of container lorries by night on roads around the Common – resulting in the choking stink of diesel fumes each morning – produced a seven-year battle from 1974. This episode brought together many people from around the Common – including the present authors.

The East Chiswick Residents' Association, 'ECRA', which includes the Chiswick area of Stamford Brook – is celebrated here in verse by one of its founder members, Yvonne Routs. It was formed in 1970 when Hounslow Borough Council threatened to demolish one house in Prebend Gardens and two in Cleveland Avenue to provide an exit from what is now Ravensmede – where an extension to the Polytechnic had been planned.

The trains had left the Goods Yard
There was nothing more to see,
The Poly hoped to build there
With car park exits three.
To do this then, the Council said,
Three houses must come down!
East Chiswick neighbours quickly sped
To spread the news around.
With pleas and supplication
Council-wards they ran.
The homes were saved! In great elation
ECRA thus began.

Yvonne Routs

Prebend Gardens soon after the great storm of 18 October 1987.
A number of the 60-year-old acacia trees fell across cars and blocked the road. A resident commented: 'It was like the Blitz! Neighbours worked together to clear the trees, and all the children in the street were playing together'

SOURCES CONSULTED:

Much of the information has been gathered from documents, unpublished manuscripts, and out-of-print books. For further information, the following is a guide to the main archives consulted and their holdings, with a short bibliography.

ARCHIVES:

Chiswick Reference Library and Local History Collection:
Rate books, council minutes, ARP Wardens' Incident Book, unpublished manuscripts, newscuttings, books, census, *Brentford & Chiswick Times* (from 1896), printed histories, directories, photographs, maps.
Hammersmith & Fulham Archives and Local History Centre:
Documents, census, rate books, deeds, maps, printed books, Sir William Bull archive, newspaper cuttings, *West London Observer* (from 1855), directories, photographs.
Acton Local History collection is housed at Ealing Central Library:
Maps, rate books, deeds, *Acton & Chiswick Gazette* (from 1871), printed histories.

Church Commissioners Records Centre 15 Galley Wall Rd, S.Bermondsey:
Records of Chiswick Prebend Estate and London Bishoprick Estate.

Ashmolean Museum, Oxford. The Pissarro Archive includes:
Diaries, sketchbooks, correspondence of Lucien, Esther and Orovida Pissarro throughout the period they lived at The Brook; all the Eragny Press books.

London Metropolitan Archives (formerly Greater London Record Office):
Metropolitan Commission for Sewers and Board of Works minute books, etc., maps, parish records, directories.

Guildhall Library:
Maps, court books for Prebend Manor, eighteenth century printed histories.

Public Record Office, Kew: Railway records of N&SWJ Railway: Reference RAIL 521, maps.

BIBLIOGRAPHY (books in print):

Bailly-Herzberg, Janine *Correspondance de Camille Pissarro* Vol.4 1895-1898 (1989)
Clegg, Gillian *Chiswick Past* (1995)
Draper, Warwick *Chiswick* (1923, reprinted 1991)
Fulham & Hamm. Hist. Soc. *A History of Hammersmith* (1965, reprinted 1990)
Harper Smith, A. & T. *The Brickfields of Acton* (1991)
Reed, Nicholas *Pissarro in West London* (1989)
Thorold, Anne ed. *The Letters of Lucien to Camille Pissarro 1883-1903* (1993)
Urbanelli, Lora *The Wood Engravings of Lucien Pissarro* Silent Books (1994)
The Victoria History of the County of Middlesex Vol.VII (1982)

Particularly useful books which are out of print:

Faulkner, Thomas *History and Antiquities of the Parish of Hammersmith* (1839)
LCC Survey of London Vol.VI Parish of Hammersmith (1915)
Meadmore, W.S. *Lucien Pissarro* W.S.Meadmore (1962)
Phillimore & Whitear *Historical Collections relating to Chiswick* (1897)
Pissarro, L.R. et Venturi, L. *Pissarro, son art, son oeuvre* (1939)
Thorold, Anne *A Catalogue of the Oil Paintings of Lucien Pissarro* (1983)

STAMFORD BROOK AND SURROUNDING AREA
1746 and 1990

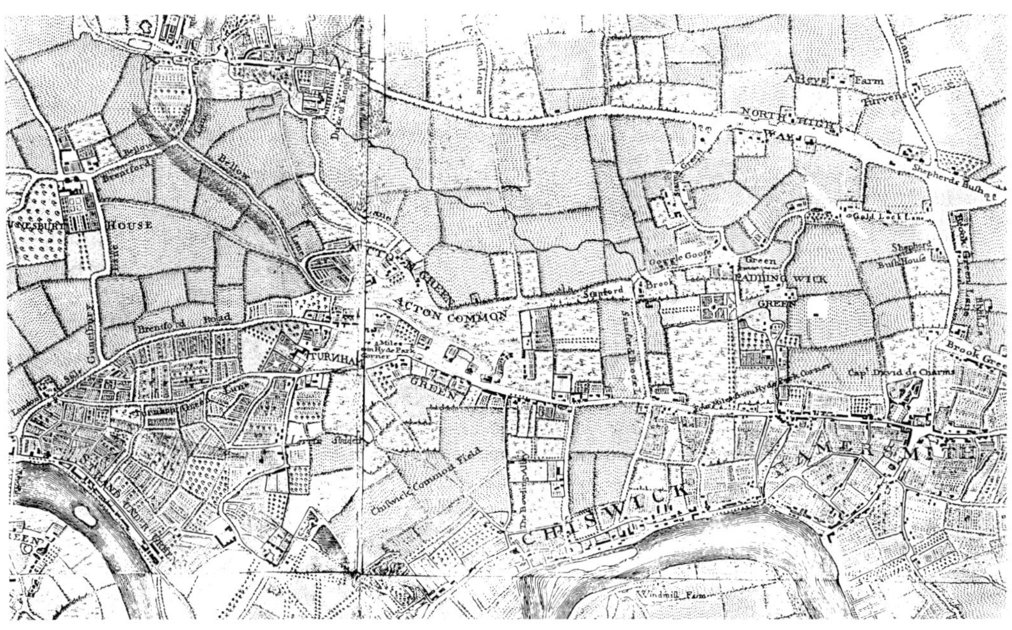

from JOHN ROCQUE's MAP 1746
Stamford brook, main branch, is shown running across fields from Acton to Stamford Brook and thence south of Padding Wick Green (through Palingswick Estate - now Ravenscourt Park) to flow into the Thames at Hammersmith Creek

from A-Z LONDON STREET ATLAS 1990
(Reproduced by permission of Geographers' A-Z Map Co.Ltd. ©Crown copyright. C4/87-05)
The Goldhawk Road/Stamford Brook Road/Bath Road follows the line of the old Roman highway

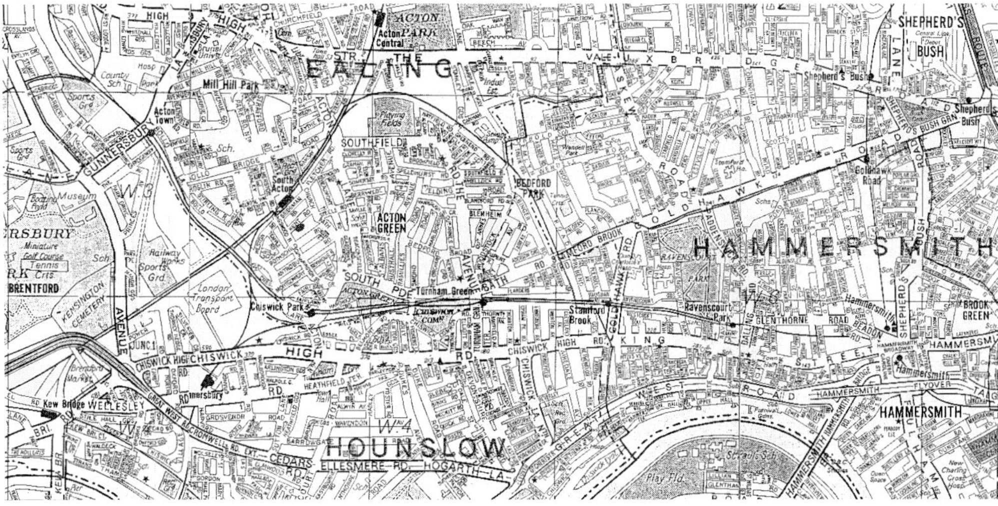

INDEX: